Our (In)visible Work: How Everyone Everywhere Experiences It Every Day

By Janelle E. Wells, Ph.D. & Doreen MacAulay, Ph.D.

Print ISBN: 979-8-9900272-9-9

Books may be purchased in bulk for educational, business, fundraising, or sales promotional use. For information, please email leader@wellsquest.com

Printed in the United States

Please note: The authors have made every effort to include the most recent website addresses. However, web addresses change over time, and the authors are not responsible for websites that are not owned by the publisher.

Our (In)visible Work
Dedications

Janelle

Mom, I see you and all the invisible work you did to raise two incredibly driven daughters as a single mother, and I thank you. You taught me how to buy the bacon, clean the bacon, cook the bacon, serve the bacon, and store the unused bacon. And I don't even eat bacon! As I stand on your shoulders, I hope to make all our work more visible.

Doreen

To Albert. Thank you for opening my eyes to questioning the status quo. You have taught me the value of each person's story in the pursuit of knowledge and a more equitable world. I will be forever grateful for your guidance and counsel.

Our (In)visible Work
Contents

Acknowledgments

Thank you to Graham Nolan for your expert guidance in bringing clarity to our vision. You make us better. We are forever grateful for our blood family and chosen family for the grace you have shown. It allowed us the space to work and create this heartfelt project. To one of the most eccentric people we know, our illustrator Galina Fouks-Abele, thank you for bringing life to our words. Finally, to the two that make the magic happen behind the curtains, Jessica Nori Johnson and Ashley Lee, without your organizational skills and deliberate encouragement this project would still be in progress.

Hope is like a road in the country. There was never a road, but when many people walk on it, the road comes into existence.
Lin Yutang, Inventor

Our (In)visible Work
Preface

WHY Our World Doesn't Exist Without Invisible Work

From the moment you wake up, there's work to be done. Your anticipation of that work may start with checking your phone for emails that arrived during your shoehorned four-hour rest. Or rummaging through your closet to find that perfect outfit. Or recalling that it is your turn again to pick up the donuts for the office. Or frantically remembering today is your child's picture day and no one else remembered or ironed their shirt last night. Some tasks become so routine you might not even see them as work anymore. Sorry to inform you: it's still work. If it takes up space in your thoughts, takes time to achieve, and makes a difference for someone, it's work, and every inch of your life is riddled with a call to action. Relationships, investments, ownerships, and hobbies are work. Families, friendships, colleagues, neighbors, pets, and children also take work.

This work is an essential part of the lives that we have created for ourselves, our families, and our communities. Knowing its value, we want to bring the weight of this work out of the shadows. Work is not always seen. In fact, what we set out to reveal in this book is how the unseen, the gaps, the unnoticed, and the expected invisible work have consequences. It also reaps gratification when the work is seen, when the work is valued, and when the work is appreciated. Work impacts our everyday life. While the impact can be relatively minor if unnoticed for a short period of time, how long can we maintain that level of work? How long can we manage

7

inevitable frustration? The frustration toward your partner for not recognizing your work for always planning the vacations, the frustration with your colleagues for always relying on you for the celebration cards, or the frustration toward your friends for always expecting you to be the social planner. Irritating, certainly. Unnoticeable, undoubtedly.

In the grand tapestry of human civilization, there exists an intricate and often unnoticed thread — our invisible work. It's the tireless unrecognized labor that underpins the functioning of our world, yet seldom receives the spotlight it deserves. From the quiet dedication of caregivers nurturing the next generation to the unsung heroes maintaining our infrastructure, invisible work is the uncelebrated backbone of our society. Without it, the world as we know it would cease to exist. It's the silent force that keeps the gears turning, the lights on, and the office lattes coming. While invisible work may not always make headlines, it forms the foundation upon which society's visible achievements are built, reminding us that the unsung efforts of countless individuals sustain the intricate web of human existence.

The global COVID-19 pandemic, with its far-reaching and profound impacts, inadvertently brought the vital but often invisible work into sharp focus. As our world grappled with the unprecedented challenges of the pandemic, it became increasingly clear that countless individuals in roles traditionally overlooked and undervalued were the unsung heroes holding society together. From healthcare professionals battling on the front lines to grocery store clerks ensuring essential supplies were available, and from teachers adapting to remote learning to caregivers providing support for the vulnerable, these dedicated individuals became the backbone of our collective resilience. Women, specifically, were three times as likely to take on all or most of the additional unpaid work when school and childcare closures occurred.[1, 2]

In addition to these essential workers, the everyday worker gained a new appreciation for the things that historically had been unseen:

- The working spouse experiencing the exhaustion of at-home child or elder care.

- The two-hour commuter utilizing the extra time to begin a new hobby.

- The new employee relieving themselves of the mental dialogue trying to meet others' expectations of their appropriate work attire.

- The token women responsible for office celebrations.

COVID-19 was a revelation, amplifying existing inequities, revealing that the fabric of our society depends not only on the conspicuous, but also on the often-hidden efforts of countless individuals and emphasizing how much our formal economy is made possible because of subsidized unpaid work. A heartbreaking reminder that behind every visible achievement stands a world of invisible work. Your invisible work. Our invisible work. Your friends' invisible work. Your colleagues' invisible work. Your parents' invisible work. The token

9

individual's invisible work. Everyone's invisible work. Now more than ever, we are deserving of recognition, respect, appreciation, and freedom.

Why We Wrote *Our (In)visible Work*

Consciously inspired by graduate students in 2016, and unconsciously instilled in me, Janelle, by my mother, my sister, my colleagues, and my husband, *Our (In)visible Work* is long overdue. As a professor hosting office hours in fall 2016, I shed tears with multiple students experiencing racist, sexist, and homophobic harassment during their graduate school internship experiences. I welcomed these students. I listened to them. I heard them. I saw them. I valued them. And I worked tirelessly meeting with their workplaces to ensure they did a better job welcoming, listening, hearing, seeing, and valuing them too. The emotional labor of handling these interactions was nothing compared to the emotional toll these individuals experienced as they were beginning their careers. Ideally, it is everyone's responsibility to make the workplace more inclusive. If you hear about a problem; it's your duty to do something about it.

Then fast forward to the height of the pandemic in summer 2020, Dr. Doreen MacAulay and I met multiple times a week as we began co-creating an online Master of Business Administration class. Although we had met one another six years prior, we were engulfed in raising children, finishing new lesson plans, and starting new jobs, but now we had focused time.

Our (In)visible Work

During the pandemic when some individuals grew more isolated, Doreen and I had the pleasure of deeply connecting. As we were ideating practical ideas to bring class content to life, we geeked out discussing management theories, research, and our own lived experiences in the academy and private sectors. I learned about Doreen's passions, her values, her dreams, and her invisible work. Together, we grew to appreciate one another's excitement for learning and helping facilitate others' learning, so we joined efforts at our consulting firm — WellsQuest — and began finalizing this book.

Our (In)visible Work stems from our own experiences of feeling that our efforts as two cisgender females working full time while raising children in North America were overlooked, particularly since the pandemic was declared. There is a sense when this happens to you that your efforts are being undervalued, that the work you do matters less, and it is this work, sometimes, that allows the others in the room to succeed with such ease. We combined our 40+ years as practitioners and scholars, aka "pracademics," who have worked in corporate settings, extended theoretical knowledge, and applied their research. Specifically, coupling our personal lived experiences with stories from teaching over 14,000 students, partnering with 150+ organizations, and leading 50+ research projects. Yes, we are two academics who have spent years trying to understand identities and inequities in the workplace, and we are repeatedly brought back to the idea that something is missing. When

Our (In)visible Work

we are looking at the issues of inequity in the workplace, there's something in the equation that we all overlook, and that part is the invisible work. This is everyday work for everyone, especially those marginalized individuals who are required to interact in any given situation.

To learn more about our personal stories, please see the About Authors section at the end of the book. This book, however, isn't about us; it is about all of us — all of *Our (In)visible Work*. Yes, there are several books that speak to the invisible work in our society, yet they mainly focus on gender as the main differentiator. What makes our book unique is the breadth of personal stories, the translational research, and the solution-oriented approaches. Throughout our work, we had so many enlightening moments hearing stories from all walks of life that we needed a moment to stop and see their work — see the beautiful work our partners do, see the restless nights our students have, see the relentless advocating our supervisors do for us, see the pain of those being triggered every day, and see the joys of life through our children's eyes.

While mainly set in a North American context, *Our (In)visible Work* is a story about bringing value and voice to all types of work. We have heard and read hundreds of your stories. And while the work discussed may have been invisible to some, the work is visible to us. Now, we want to help be a vessel to make these stories visible to all. To remind everyone, you especially, that your work matters. Throughout this journey, we will explore invisible work that happens in the public and private sectors of our lives to provide strategies to make it more visible.

Statistics Reveal the Invisible Work

The statistics on invisible work highlight the disparities that persist in our society. According to a study by the Organization for Economic Cooperation and Development (OECD), women shoulder a disproportionate burden, dedicating an average of 4.5 hours per day to unpaid work, while men contribute 2.5 hours.[3, 4] Similarly, reports from the United Nations (UN)[3] and Harvard Business Review[1] highlight that women globally perform 75% of unpaid care and domestic labor, reflecting an imbalance that impacts women's economic and personal lives.

Popularized and gamified as household management or life admin,[5, 6, 7] unpaid care includes anything from cooking, cleaning, organizing, scheduling, childcare, and elder care.[1] Even in professional settings, women are frequently burdened with "office housework," undertaking tasks that often go unnoticed like planning lunches, ordering food, recognizing birthdays, and decorating for holidays.

Whether in professional and personal spheres, there is also a gendered nature of emotional labor (discussed in chapter 2), as women are often tasked with and evaluated on managing emotions and relationships. The taxing, and often unseen, work of editing your emotions to influence someone else's emotional state is not limited to women.[8, 9, 10, 11, 12, 13, 14]

Throughout history researchers have indicated Black individuals often navigate stereotype management,[9, 10] Latin individuals regularly combat immigrant status stigmas,[11, 12] and Asian individuals encounter cultural expectation norms to behave passively,[13, 14] all forms of emotional labor, which adds an extra layer of responsibility. Considering these historical racial, gender, and cultural imbalances, it's not surprising that a workforce revolution is brewing. According to the Rosie Report 70% of Gen Z (people born between ~1997-2012) are contemplating earning extra income outside their current employers, and particularly marginalized groups are expressing a stronger desire for hybrid work options to address these systemic disparities.[15]

Setting the Stage for Discussion

To navigate the complexities surrounding invisible work there is a need to bring awareness to the hijacking of terms. So, to set the stage for a discussion that we can all engage in, let us level-set and share a common vocabulary for your journey throughout this book contextualizing the following:

Invisible Work

All work, physical or mental, that's done for someone else without acknowledgement of the time, effort, or contribution of the work. The parentheses around (in)visible work in our book title is purposeful because there is always someone for whom this work is visible in the workload they carry or the stress they experience.

Gender

Once seen as a binary concept, is now recognized as a complex and multifaceted spectrum that encompasses a wide range of identities and experiences. At its core, gender refers to the roles, behaviors, and expectations that society assigns to individuals based on their perceived identity.[16] However, it is essential to understand that gender is not simply a matter of biology. It is deeply intertwined with culture, history, expression, and identification.

Importantly, throughout this book, gender is addressed socially through a binary lens (i.e., woman and man) because we are sharing our own experiences, our institutionalized history, and the experiences of those who volunteered as part of our research. However, we want to recognize that gender inequity extends to gender expansive and gender fluid. Throughout history and culture, power has been categorized primarily through a binary structure where "see[ing] men as the human default is fundamental to the structure of human society."[17] Also, the word "men," as author Caroline Criado Perez[17] notes in *Invisible Women: Data Bias in a World Designed for Men*, has been universal for "White men." Now White men, keep reading, we are calling you in: You have invisible work, and we need you in this conversation and on this journey so we can all help one another turn the invisible visible.

15

Our (In)visible Work

Intersectionality

In our complex and diverse world, it is imperative to see the interconnected nature of identities and how social categorizations create various forms of inequality (discussed in chapter 6). Incorporating an intersectional perspective in our book is important to broaden perspectives. Additionally, we refrain from using "women" as code for "White women" and "men" as universal for "White men," which would erroneously ignore other social identities.

Understanding intersectionality requires a unique way of thinking because of the additive way identities operate, not standing alone.

Self-Care

In our fast-paced, demanding world that often glorifies endless productivity and self- sacrifice, the concept of self-care has emerged as a beacon of hope and resilience. It is the declaration that "I matter and so does my well-being." Self-care is a deliberate and mindful practice of taking care of your own physical, mental, and emotional health. Recognize your own worthiness, declare that your needs matter, and act with compassion toward yourself. In essence, self-care is not a selfish act but a selfless one. You know the instructions when you board an airplane — "Put on your own oxygen mask before assisting others," so let's practice the same in our daily lives.

Allyship

In our increasingly interconnected world, allyship has gained prominence. Allyship is an empathetic and proactive stance that individuals or groups of individuals take to support others, often marginalized or oppressed people and communities. It is a commitment to stand in solidarity with others, amplify their voices, and actively work to dismantle systems of inequity. Partnering to acknowledge that we share a common humanity and that liberating one group is intertwined with the liberation of all. Allyship is not passive; it is a conscious decision to act.

What the World Would Be Without Invisible Work

In a world without invisible labor, the fabric of our daily lives would unravel. This often- overlooked force, which silently but tirelessly keeps the gears of society turning, is the uncelebrated backbone of our civilization. Its absence would reverberate in countless ways, profoundly altering the very fabric of our existence. Imagine a world where caregivers, often women, no longer perform the invisible labor of nurturing families and maintaining homes. The emotional support provided — countless meals prepared, medicine administered, education instructed, and care given — would suddenly become conspicuous by their absence. The impacts would cascade, affecting the well-being and productivity of every member of society.

Moreover, in a world without the invisible labor of countless individuals who maintain critical infrastructure, our lives would grind to a halt. In essence, a world without invisible labor would be chaotic and dysfunctional. It would starkly reveal the immense contributions of those

Our (In)visible Work

whose efforts often remain hidden. It would underscore that the intricate web of human existence relies not just on visible achievements but also on the countless, often unsung actions of individuals working tirelessly behind the scenes.

It is our hope then, through this work, not to alleviate invisible work, because the work must get done. We hope, rather, to bring the invisible work out of the shadows where it can be acknowledged, valued, and respected for what it is — work.

Ignorance is the source of hatred, and the way to get rid of ignorance is realization.
Dalai Lama, Buddhist Leader

Our (In)visible Work
Introduction

WHERE Invisible Work Lives — and How to See It

In 1977, French sociologist Pierre Bourdieu wrote, "What is essential goes without saying because it comes without saying: The tradition is silent, not least about itself as a tradition."[1] The silent work that you have routinely been doing daily, for years, maybe even for decades, is invisible to others because it has become implicitly your default or others' expectation. Invisible work is silent precisely because it needs to be localized. It is tasks that are implicit, unquestioned, defaulted, expected — particularly for anyone who is used to completing these tasks in a system not designed by them or for them.

To better understand these invisible work issues, unpack the challenges they create, and share strategies people have used to bring attention to their work, we went to what we know best: researching the history and interviewing people about the concept of work that goes unrecognized and undervalued, both inside and outside of the home. While interviewee's names have been changed to honor their vulnerability in sharing their stories, there are three descriptors (age, career interest, and a humanizing hashtag) provided to contextualize their experience. After two decades of award-winning research and six years of conversation with hundreds of people, we started to have a good sense of the trends in people's professional and personal lives. Throughout the book, we distill personal stories for 27 different people sharing eye-opening situations and

Our (In)visible Work

a variety of impactful research and approaches for a brighter future.

As students of social constructionism, we believe that through personal stories and experiences we can better appreciate the underlying issues that need to be surfaced for sustainable change to occur. From this we believe there is always an opportunity for every individual to evaluate and navigate the realities that society creates for them as individuals and as part of a system. For example, how has the concept of families evolved over time? The word *family* may not even resonate with those that have not had a formative experience. It has been socially constructed with each passing generation, so the roles of people of different genders, ages, educational levels, experiences, and even the interactions with people outside of the family are all the design of the society in which individuals live. To be active agents in that design, however, we need to first be able to understand it.

The notion of work alone, set apart from the rest of life, is a peculiarly Western idea. Even after enduring a pandemic as life became integrated, making a distinction between work and life was darn near impossible. Over the last four decades even, economic and social transformations have altered our work, life, and family structures. Although these structures are evolving from patriarchal to egalitarian, unique changes have occurred — from the emergence of 24/7 technological access with convenient user-friendly tablets and smartphones, to integrated flexible work systems and households with the highest number of single-parent and dual-earning homes.[2, 3, 4, 5] Since the 1970s, the percentage of U.S. families that have both parents working increased from 49% to 66% of households.[6] Even in hetero-coupled households where women are high-wage earners, sometimes higher than their husbands, a portion of the women's uncounted and unpaid labor was tailoring their work to fit the circumstances.[7] For examples, the majority of women are leaving early in the afternoon to pick up the children, working remotely when a child is ill, or starting the work day earlier to be able to chaperon the school field trip. Such examples of the invisible work of tailoring reinforces, whether consciously or unconsciously, the gendered expectations and separations reminding us that we live in a society not designed by or for us. Guess it's time to redesign?

Coined by sociologist Arlene Kaplan Daniels in the 1980s,[7] "invisible work" is described as forms of unpaid labor, generally for women, like volunteer work or housework that, while integral for a functioning society, is not regarded as work and is too often culturally and economically devalued, if valued at all. For the purposes of our work, we want to expand the interpretation of this construct. Invisible work is all work that's done for someone else without acknowledgement of the time, effort, or contribution of the work. In studying this topic, we have learned there is much invisible work that people expect from colleagues, family, friends, and neighbors that we need to start identifying if we want to better understand efforts. In the workplace, invisible work has manifested as office housework. In the home, bloggers have labeled it as life admin.[8, 9]

Yet in our social lives, what do we call this work?

As the North American society experiences record numbers of burnout, we need to uncover what is at the heart of the burnout. Wellness programs, mindfulness training, and improved health routines may attempt to alleviate these issues, but are they dealing with the symptoms of a system that needs alteration? If we think of the work of scholars like Anthony C. Klotz and Mark C. Bolino,[10] who are credited with predicting the Great Resignation, there are clues of how work is not always properly compensated. And that there is an imbalance in what work is valued. Their study into the dark side of organizational citizenship behavior highlights that the additional discretionary tasks often described as going above and beyond are not inherently bad or good, but their impact needs to be further studied.

Invisible Work Lives in Your Roles

The roles we play in society often come with unspoken expectations. As two married cisgender females working full time as professors and part-time as consultants all while raising children and assisting aging parents, there are a significant amount of the discussions centered around identities and gender issues. And while we know that globally women, compared to men, do three times the amount of unpaid care work at home, on top of the childcare and housework,[11] this book is not solely focused on gender. *Everyone* has invisible work. In the transformative state that our society is experiencing, we all must be part of the conversation to realign the workplace to be a place where people's talents or their time are not taken advantage of because of a part of their identity. In addition to our identities, some of the most profound roles often carry the weight of invisible work — those quiet, unsung tasks that go beyond the surface and shape the very essence of our existence. For example:

- **The token individual**: The invisible work of the token individual in the workplace is a subtle but a weighty burden to bear. Beyond the visible tasks and responsibilities, this individual often shoulders the unspoken societal expectation to represent an entire demographic. It is the quiet effort to navigate biases, dispel stereotypes, and pave the way for others who may follow. It involves the emotional labor of constantly managing expectations, educating colleagues, and advocating for oneself and others. The token individual often finds themself in the role of an ambassador for diversity and inclusion, serving as a living example of what is possible, all while managing their regular workload.

- **The stay-at-home parent**: The invisible work of a stay-at-home parent is a symphony of love and dedication, orchestrated behind the scenes of daily life. It extends far beyond visible tasks. It's the emotional labor of constantly answering the question, what do you do all day? It's the management of schedules, doctor's appointments, and playdates, often executed with meticulous precision. It's the juggling act of maintaining a harmonious household, keeping the family's needs met, and providing a nurturing environment where love and learning thrive. This invisible work is a labor of profound significance, shaping not only the lives of children but also the bonds that tie a family together, and it deserves the recognition and appreciation it often humbly foregoes.

- **The cultural translator**: The invisible work of being the person others look to educate, translate, connect, and enhance communications between different cultures. You may not be the lone individual of a group. You may not even be part of the group you are translating for, however, through your experience, language abilities, cultural knowledge, or empathetic nature you are expected to be a communication conduit continuing to make things *hum* in the office.

From these examples we see the potential layers of invisible work that people are experiencing. Adhering to the idea that once you have seen something you cannot unsee it, one would believe that acknowledgement of the unseen work would be enough to initiate change. The norms and expectations of roles, however, are steeped in culture, religion, and a strong history and make the want for change

25

insufficient. There needs to be more deliberate and intentional action.

Invisible Work: A Loose Thread

Think of our invisible work, as a loose thread — an unraveled strand of our carefully woven existence. Like a single loose thread, it may seem insignificant at first, easily dismissed or overlooked. However, if left unattended, it has the potential to unravel the entire fabric of our lives. Considering invisible work as the loose thread requires acknowledging the impact of invisible work on people that are expected to live up to certain role expectations. Increased rates of burnout and unhappiness suggest we need to consider the loose thread. As we confront the concept of invisible work, we have several choices in how we want to deal with the loose thread. Leaning into the thread metaphor — how have you dealt with a loose thread on a piece of clothing? Did you:

- Let it be and fray further — risking the unraveling of what we hold dear.
- Tug at it — seeking to repair.
- Cut it off — putting an end to it.

Option one: Let it be. Continue the frustration of invisible work. We may choose to ignore the loose thread, hoping it will not be noticed or eventually fade into obscurity. This path can offer temporary relief, allowing us to avoid discomfort or confrontation. However, it carries the risk of the loose thread growing longer and more troublesome over time. What initially seemed inconsequential might become a source of frustration, regret, resentment, or missed opportunity.

Option two: Tug at it. Find a way to get invisible work compensated, valued, seen as a means of beginning to repair the imbalance of activity. This choice involves facing the loose thread head-on, acknowledging its presence, and taking action to address it. We might engage in introspection, seeking to understand why the loose thread exists and what it represents in our lives. This process can be both uncomfortable and enlightening, as we may uncover hidden emotions, unresolved issues, or neglected aspirations. Tugging at the loose thread can lead to personal growth and healing, allowing us to mend the fabric of our lives.

Option three: Cut it off. Stop doing the invisible work. In this case, acceptance and self-compassion can be powerful choices. In some cases, one needs to set themself free from the invisible work. Instead of tugging at the loose thread or constantly trying to repair it, free yourself of the frustration. We want to be clear, however, that we believe sometimes people do have to free themselves yet realize all of us cannot free ourselves of all invisible work because a lot of it is imperative for our existence. More on that later.

Ultimately, the presence of invisible work, a loose thread in the fabric of our lives, is a reminder of our humanity — an invitation to explore, reflect, and make choices. Whether we choose to ignore, mend, or free ourselves, the act of acknowledging the loose thread is a step toward understanding ourselves and others and the intricacies of human existence. It is through these choices that we continue to weave the rich tapestry of our life's journey.

Exploring a Pop Cultural Understanding of Invisible Work

Invisible work is a pop cultural phenomenon. The pandemic was a tipping point for a lot of individuals, especially for those that are newer to the workplace, who were no longer willing to work for free. Changes have been happening for years, but the idea gained new attention during and since the pandemic. As an example, in the context of the U.S. school systems, obtaining an internship (unpaid or paid), has been an integral part of the work culture.

Historically, working for free was a rite of passage, but times have changed. Profits have grown. People have evolved. Internships have changed and the labor laws surrounding internships have evolved over time. In 1938, U.S. labor legislation of the Fair Labor Standards Act (FLSA) originally did not provide clear guidelines for unpaid internships.[12, 13] Instead, it focused on distinguishing between employees and trainees. Then in 2010, the Department of Labor (DOL) issued new guidelines to clarify when internships could be unpaid under the FLSA. Eight years later, in 2018, further clarifications were made to the criteria for unpaid internship, including the "primary beneficiary" test focusing on whether the intern or the employer was the primary beneficiary of the relationship. If the intern received the greater benefit, the internship could be unpaid.[12]

Our (In)visible Work

We continued this exploration for avenues of change in work culture. In some situations, change is disguised as opportunities where individuals are exploited. For example, in 2023, the entertainment industry made headlines as the Screen Actors Guild (SAG) and the Writers Guild of America (WGA) embarked on a highly publicized strike. This strike was a culmination of simmering tensions and long-standing disputes between these influential guilds and the major film and television studios. The primary point of contention revolved around compensation, recognition of work, and fair treatment for professionals in the industry and the work. SAG and WGA members were advocating for more equitable wages, improved working conditions, and better healthcare and retirement benefits. They argued that despite the booming streaming industry and record-breaking box office revenues, their share of the profits had not kept pace with the industry's growth. The strike, which garnered widespread attention in both entertainment and mainstream news, led to disruptions in film and television production schedules. Several high-profile projects were put on hold, and many popular TV shows faced delays in production, leaving fans eagerly awaiting their return.

As contentious as some of these situations may seem, these are the types of conversations that need to happen for us to truly understand and bring light to the invisible work in our society.

Our (In)visible Work

Get Ready to Unravel

Of the options of how to deal with this thread of invisible work, we are opting for the route of tug and repair. Throughout this book we will take you on a journey to understand some of the themes that arose from the hundreds of conversations we had with people from various professions in various positions in various industries. We have categorized the book into four parts: when, what, who, and how. First, we start with *when*, sharing some of the reasons when invisible work is present. Second, we move into *what*, describing some ways invisible work materializes. Third, we discuss *who* can help reshape the invisible economy. Finally, we call everyone to action describing *how* we can make invisible work visible. At the end of every chapter there is a conclusion section entitled *mirrors*. The mirrors are solution-oriented calls for you to look in the mirror or possibly hold a mirror up to someone else. We hope this book will help people better understand the work in their own lives that is unseen and the way in which it manifests within them while working to make it visible to others.

There is peace in highlighting the need for understanding. There is hope in sharing these stories, too, because when we can step out of our own heads, speak up for ourselves, and advocate for others, then change can begin. People awaken and take notice. And so, at heart, *Our (In)visible Work* is a call for change. Today, right now, let's do the work to make the change together!

Part 1: WHEN Invisible Work Becomes Visible Behavior

Every truth we see is one to give to the world, not to keep to ourselves alone.
Elizabeth Dacy Stanton, Women's Rights Leader

Chapter 1

When Relationships Affect Authenticity and Adaptability

Our (In)visible Work
1: When Relationships Affect Authenticity and Adaptability

Have you ever thought:

"I cannot believe what I am hearing." And made the choice to say nothing?

"I cannot miss my specialist appointment." And yet stayed at work to make a deadline?

"If I speak up, I'll rock the boat." And chose to stay silent for peace?

"If I continue to do this, I will burnout." And still haven't changed anything?

Well, the good thing is you're in good company. And the bad thing is you're in good company. You are not alone. Understanding how to balance between being your authentic self and adapting to your situation is a struggle that a lot of people have experienced. As we have learned from working on this project, people are starting to embrace pieces of their identity more fully, and as such, are working to find ways to ensure their voice, work, and contributions are seen. By embracing their authentic self, they are reducing and alleviating the invisible work required in hiding or muting pieces of themselves.

Being Our Authentic Selves Means Assessing Your Roles and Identities

Authenticity is rare, yet ideal. Authenticity is a concept that refers to being genuine, true to oneself, and transparent in one's actions, beliefs, and interactions.[1] It involves aligning one's behaviors, values, and expressions with their innermost feelings and convictions, rather than conforming to external expectations or pressures.[2] As industrial organizational scholar Adam Grant[3] clarifies, "Authenticity is not about expressing every opinion you hold. It's about ensuring that what you voice reflects what you value."

Personally and professionally, authenticity is a potent catalyst for success. Allowing you to connect on a deeper level and foster stronger interpersonal relationships and better teamwork. Moreover, when people are authentic, they tend to be more confident and self-assured, enabling them to take on challenges with a sense of purpose and conviction. Authenticity also invites innovation, as individuals are more likely to share unique perspectives and ideas when they feel safe to do so. When individuals bring their genuine selves, it creates an environment conducive to trust and collaboration.

Before opening to authenticity, the concept of identity needs to be explored. Identity is a complex concept with a variety of facets. A person's identity is a collection of characteristics and traits that influence who they are as a person. Literature in this area ranges from a deterministic view that identity is stable to a constructionist view of the continuous state of development and alteration as we have lived experiences.[4] There have been dissertations discussing this topic (including one of the authors — go Dr. MacAulay!), but for our purposes here, we want to focus on the constructionist view of identity and consider how our roles and values

35

influence the continual formation of identity. This focus is inspired by the amazing stories people shared with us about how they have had to hide or suppress parts of their identity to achieve their goals or to simply be accepted.

Adapting Our Roles and Identities to Uphold Relationships

Adaptability is the ability to adjust, change, or modify oneself in response to new circumstances, challenges, or environments. It involves the capacity to embrace change, learn from experiences, and effectively navigate evolving situations. Adaptability encompasses flexibility, resilience, and the willingness to explore innovative solutions when faced with unexpected or changing conditions. As we piloted the invisible work interview questions as part of this overall project, the first question originally stated, "Select how often you spend time and energy completing these tasks in the workplace." One of our stay-at-home parents, Ivy, promptly informed us, "Maybe this survey doesn't apply to me, so I shouldn't take this survey." Immediately, we clarified with her that her workplace is everywhere.

It is amazing how one simple word revealed a great deal about Ivy's own perception of self and the perception society has cast upon her as a stay-at-home parent. In actuality, she is volunteering over 30 hours a month at her church and at her children's school in addition to assisting with elder care, so one could not convince us that she does not work. But in many ways, society has told her that these efforts do not amount to work

36

because she does not get compensated by an organization. What a powerful discussion that helped us ensure there were not more people thinking these ideals did not pertain to them. As such, we define the workplace as any work or non-leisure activity, outside of the home, whether paid or unpaid.

The Complexity of Defining Work

Whether it is in or outside of the workplace, people struggle with defining work, first, and then valuing work. Value is a constructed term that means different things to different people. In our modern, cash nexus, industrialized society, one of the most common understandings of work is that it is a task, duty, or assignment for which you get paid. Even though the pay was not equitable, being paid for one's time as an employee is a concept popularized in the late 1760s during the Industrial Revolution.[5] To earn money — to "work" — has historically been an indicator of one's status, unless you were aristocracy. Working was a way to develop a sense of self-esteem and a sense of identity. Researchers have tried to distinguish work from leisure activities (bass fishing, knitting, or following Pearl Jam across the world) and personal activities (homemaking and romantic relationships). Society's idealizing the separation of work from personal activities caused even more concern for the division of labor when men went out to the public world to work, and women remained at home in the private world to raise the family. Archaic, yes. Realistic, yes. Yet work is broader than the accomplishments for which we are paid. Historically, even public activities like volunteering were not considered work if they were not compensated.

To explore how these narrow definitions of work are unrealistic, let us look at Ivy's invisible work as a stay-at-home parent who is constantly working to serve others.

You do work 24 hours a day, especially when you have newborns or toddlers. The work never stops. And you have so many different hats you wear and roles you play being a stay-at-home [parent] that you don't necessarily get recognition, even by your own peers or family, and then as, you know, as a woman and your insecurities may flare. You tend to question your worth a lot. You know, sometimes we also feel like Uber drivers. Every day, you're having to take the kids to school. You're picking them up from school, taking them to sport practices or maintaining their social life. Then you're the tutor, you're the volunteer art teacher, you're also the cook and the server. And then you put the coach hat on for whatever sport they are doing, and then back in the Uber. Then you come home and you're the chef and server again for your spouse, and then you've got to be the nurturing caretaker for not only the kids but our aging parents. It's just, it's emotionally draining at times because we rarely get recognized for our work. You also tend to lose yourself as a woman, as a spouse, as a person because you are constantly playing all these different roles, yet society continues to ask me, 'what do you do all day?'

Ivy. 40s. Stay-at-Home Mom. #PuertoRicanPrincess

Our (In)visible Work

Even in our twenty-first century egalitarian society, women are doing twice as much childcare and housework compared to their male counterparts. According to the International Labour Organization's World Employment and Social Outlook study,[6] women spend two more hours of their time daily on "unpaid care and domestic work" compared to their male counterparts.[6, 7, 8] Even prior to the pandemic, women did 75% of the world's unpaid care work.[8] In 2022, McKinsey & Company estimated the value of unpaid care carried out by women contributed $10 trillion to annual global GDP.[9] Three stories of invisible work from Kristen, Amber, and Patti bring this data to life, as they reflect on negotiating their roles between work, childcare, and home. Listen to Kristen negotiating her invisible work with her desire for self- care.

> Since becoming a so-called "working mom," I have had to constantly think about when I can fit my exercise routine into my family and work schedule. Do I have to do it in the morning before the house wakes up? Before making breakfast? Or the lunches? Is it too dark then for me to go running outside by myself? But I can't go after work. I need to prepare dinner and help the kids with homework, and I can't go after the kids go to sleep because, again, it's too dark or I want to spend time with my partner. Oh, forget it, I just won't do it today.
>
> **Kristen. 50s. Government Employee. #YogaLover**

Managing the work of mom and house with her personal wellness goals is constant work. Next, Amber notes her invisible work preparing the household for her work trip.

> Whenever I prepare for a work trip, I organize suppers. I prep meals. I draft up a schedule for my husband even though we already have a shared calendar. I ensure that bills are paid. I even ensure the kids' clothes are laid out for the week. However, when he leaves the house for a work trip, he just leaves.
>
> **Amber. 40s. Finance Director. #OnlyChildCaretaker**

Now some may say this is a personal challenge, handle it with your partner. However, societal expectation shave creeped into intimate partnerships and continue to set unrealistic demands of women. Although there are still only 24 hours in a day, and more and more women are in the workforce, societal expectations have not evolved.

Not only is invisible work present in workday preparation, but it is also present for a number of people at their workplace. Let's look at Patti's invisible work of preparing to celebrate a colleague's birthday.

> Tell me the last time my male colleagues remembered a birthday, bought a birthday card, or made a cake. Shoot, *bought* a cake. Now, when I ask them for money, they do contribute to the gift; however, why do I always have to ask? You know every year on this day, it is a birthday.

How about they mark their calendar too?

Patti. 30s. Business Developer. #SingleWorldTraveler

Patti's reflection is so relatable to those who regularly organize the office birthday celebrations, happy hours, or socials. The research shows the value of these types of activities for organizational culture and creating a positive work climate; however, the tasks are never formally assigned and are left to be done by the nurturing types, or the "ones that like that sort of thing." It is the unseen activities that create the invisible work that so many take on in addition to their everyday workload.

Invisible work can also surface through expectations placed on people because of other pieces of their identity like tenure in a position, religion, ability, ethnicity, gender identity, marital or parental status. To further explore all the places invisible work lives, let us consider Jeremy, Andy, Kevin, and Joy's stories.

Gotta love being one of the only single individuals in my department, maybe even across my organization at this management level. So when a last-minute need arises, guess who always gets asked and is expected to help? Yeah, you know I don't have a partner to get home to. I don't have kids to go pick up. Yeah, guess I don't have a life either.

Jeremy. 30s. Experience Curator. #QueerBrit

Like Jeremy, Andy's invisible work came in the form of always feeling

41

like he had to be available to fill in for others, particularly because he didn't have a partner or children.

> Yes, I am young, single, and childless; however, that doesn't mean I am always the emergency call every time there is a last-minute ask. Even though I have an active life, I'm consistently guilted for saying "no" or "I can't help."
>
> **Andy. 20s. Analytics Coordinator. #NumberNerd**

Both Jeremy and Andy's invisible work revealed itself when they would adapt their single-life schedule to meet other's demands, and then feeling judged when they did create a boundary. Next, let's consider Kevin's invisible work of maintaining his authenticity as he prepares to attend a conference. He wants to be authentic; however, this is his first academic conference, so he knows it is the start of the interview process coupled with first impressions in a majority population.

> Recently, I was attending my first academic conference, and I was nervous about what to wear and how to present myself. My advisor's advice — it is pretty casual, you'll be fine. I thought that really wasn't an answer, so I called my older sister and asked what I should do? How should I style my hair? What should I wear? She suggested I keep my dreads tight and select modest colors and professional attire.
>
> **Kevin. 20s. Doctoral Student. #HaitianArtist**

Our (In)visible Work

This story highlights the potential influence of professionalism to mute authenticity and identity, which many have to balance and define for themselves. We will talk more about this later in the book. Finally, we've done the invisible work, preparing for work and now maybe we're leaving the workplace for the day. Let's look at Joy's work of bringing visibility to someone else's work.

I do this exercise in class: I ask everyone to write down what they think about when leaving a building late at night. Of the diverse population present, some people have a list of 15+ thoughts, while others list "nothing." It's a great exercise for others to see some of the work spent thinking: Do I call someone? Do I stay off the phone, so I'm not distracted? Do I share my pin drop? Do I keep my hair down or put it in a ponytail? Do I hold onto my purse or hide it in my bag? Do I keep my keys out, so I have easy access to opening the car? And have my pepper spray in hand? Do I make noise, so others know I'm behind them? Do I cross the street, so others don't think I'm following them?

Joy. 40s. Professor. #LatinaBoyMom

Mirrors

Together, these stories remind us that invisible work is everywhere and occurs every day. As we work to bring light to invisible work, one must recognize that **there is no us versus them.** You are them. We are them. Everyone has some form of invisible work, and together we

43

can help bring visibility. One specific way to bring visibility is by **fostering conversations.** Start by asking someone what tasks they recently accomplished that may have gone unnoticed. Also take a moment to reflect on your own invisible contributions and share your thoughts to create dialogue. If people do not know the work that is being completed, then it is naïve to expect them to see the work that is being done. Now is not the time to be bashful. It is the time to courageously and confidently bring visibility to the invisible. **Unapologetically share your story.** Proudly discuss your work, the impact of your contributions, and the value of your work. Connect the dots for folks. Goodness, why do I have to do more work? Redundant, possibly. Helpful, incredibly. Remember everyone walks a different path and has a different viewpoint. Through conversations, we ask that you take the opportunity to vividly share your perspective.

Our (In)visible Work

Emotions are much like waves: We can't stop them from coming, but we can choose which one to surf.
Anonymous

Chapter 2
When Emotional Labor Becomes Visible

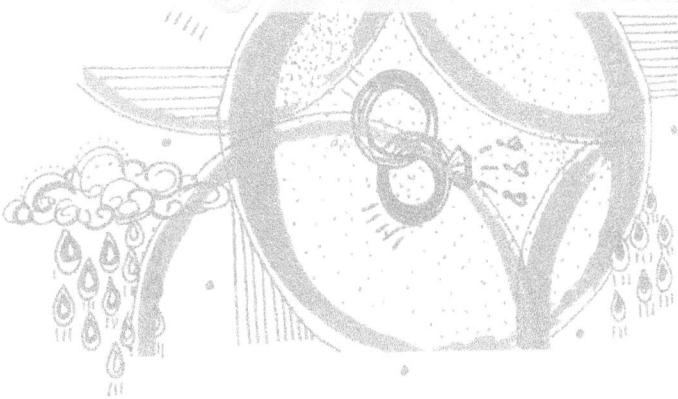

2: When Emotional Labor Becomes Visible

Have you ever had to bite your tongue:

- **To save face?**

- **To maintain control?**

- **To protect someone?**

Have you ever had to disguise feeling overwhelmed:

- **To meet a deadline?**

- **To care for someone else?**

- **To make it through the day?**

If you answered yes to any of the questions above, you have experienced emotional labor. It takes emotional labor to process, feel, and regulate oneself. Many of the people that we interviewed during this project spoke about having to monitor their behavior in specific situations to be able to remain civil or to act in accordance with societal expectations. This is work, invisible work. More specifically, it is something called emotional labor. It is the type of labor you cannot see or quantify but that takes conscious cognitive effort and can be exhausting. The theme of emotional labor surfaced during this project in a variety of ways. There were some people we spoke with who talked about workplace interactions that required regulation, others talked about issues specific to race and gender, while others spoke to the invisible work of being a good partner, colleague, family member, and friend. We will explore these different manifestations of emotional labor in this chapter.

48

Our (In)visible Work

Before we begin to understand emotional labor and the role it plays in creating invisible work for us, let's first understand emotions and emotional displays. For simplicity's sake, emotion is a mental state usually displayed in three forms: integrative, differentiating, and masking.[1] Integrative emotions are generally hedonically positive, and they create good feelings and encourage harmony (e.g., compassion, love, and happiness) between people. Think of how you might feel compassion, love, or happiness when you have lunch with a dear friend. Conversely, differentiating emotions are noted as hedonically negative and tend to drive a wedge between people (e.g., anger, fear, hate). Think of that disagreement you had with a neighbor about a zoning vote affecting your children's school. You might have stormed home angry, fearful, or hateful. And finally, there is masking, which is when an individual takes a neutral position demonstrative of neither integrative nor differentiating emotions.[2] Think of masking as the ticketing agent who is getting yelled at for something completely out of their control yet having to remain calm and pleasant to the customer. This happens especially in the service industry, where organizations train employees to adhere to integrative emotional display rules, whether they are servicing external or internal customers.

With these definitions in mind, think of your own experience: How many times today have you displayed emotions that contradicted your genuine emotions, thus prompting a discrepancy between the emotion you felt and the emotion displayed? This is typical. This is work

— actual invisible work. This causes an emotional dissonance or having to meet external expectations with a differing felt emotion from the expressed emotion. As it is something that most people do on a regular basis, it does not mean that the impacts and the ramifications of this dissonance should be ignored. People need to be able to acknowledge the mental effort needed to complete these types of interactions and find outlets for their stress. If the interactions are consistent over time and still not addressed, it can be harmful to a person's physical and psychological well-being. Just because effort is unseen, we cannot ignore the stress, exhaustion, and toll it can take on us.

The term "emotional labor" comes from sociology literature. In the book, *Emotional Labor in the 21st Century*,[3] psychologist Alicia Grandey and organizational psychologist Allison Gabriel state that emotional labor is "invisible work done by one person to quell the needs or demands of others, both in the workplace and in social and domestic situations." The idea of "emotion work" was first coined in the 1980s by sociologist Arlie Russell Hochschild[4] in her book, *The Managed Heart: Commercialization of Human Feeling.* She defined what we now call emotional labor as "the management of feelings to create a publicly observable facial and bodily display." Hochschild focused on the workplace, describing how employees must regulate their emotional states as part of their job requirement. Whether dealing with that angry customer or holding in your devastation of bad news in front of colleagues, the emotional state of the worker is to be suitable. Khalil recalls how and why he was taught to regulate his emotions in the workplace.

> As a Black man, I've been taught to control my emotions, especially in the workplace, because if you do show emotion, it will be misconstrued as something other than what it is — passion. Instead, it will be labeled aggression or insubordination. I've always been cautioned to stay away, keep your rapport, keep your poise, bite your tongue in certain situations. Or even not bite your tongue but rephrase what you really wanted to say because suddenly, I'm the aggressor.
>
> **Khalil. 40s. Operations Executive. #GirlDad**

Today, 40 years after Hochschild book's publication, the concept still applies to both personal and professional relationships, generally referencing the invisible work it takes to manage one's emotions and well-being to achieve societal norms. To handle situations with emotional labor, there is a required amount of effort, as well as planning and anticipation needed to express socially desirable emotions during interpersonal transactions.[5, 6] If people acknowledge, anticipate, and plan for this emotional labor, they can alleviate the stress from the given situation. Many workplaces try to help this by providing training on how to deal with difficult conversations and behaviors to ensure you have time to debrief with a trusted friend or colleague after the emotional interaction.

One person we spoke with said they scheduled a break after each planned interaction with a specific colleague. This colleague's condescending nature and argumentative approach meant the person had to demonstrate restraint when engaging. Having felt the impact of the toxic environment, the individual finally developed coping mechanisms to deal with the emotional labor of these interactions. The person would take time to walk and process the conversation allowing themselves to feel the emotions that were not expressed during the encounter. Now, yes, every relationship involves some level of emotional work, whether it is caring for a friend who is feeling down or trying to respectfully articulate your emotions while disagreeing with your partner. The key, however, is to understand when the emotional labor is draining you and ensure you are finding a mechanism to address your true emotions.

Originally, Hochschild[4] intended the term emotional labor as "work, for which you're paid, which centrally involves trying to feel the right feeling for the job." Again, we go back to the limited definition of "work" as an action that's compensated with payment including having to be paid. **Sociology scholar Amy S. Wharton,**[1] however, noted that such work is not only paid, but also under the control of other individuals. Hochschild[4] looked at the labor division between the feelings we experience and the expression of feelings that we are supposed to be portraying to the world. Imagine servicing a disrespectful retail customer with a smile or being a flight attendant graciously telling the thousandth resistant customer not to unbuckle their seatbelt.

Our (In)visible Work

Laura, a college professor, reminisces on several discussions about the emotional toll it takes managing her emotions as she serves her disrespectful students.

> Emotional labor isn't listed in my job description, but I have noticed it has become a majority of my work. These days, there are such high expectations of me, and I'd say most female faculty, to emotionally support students. It takes a tremendous amount of effort to serve them. Even when some are blatantly disrespectful, they still expect me to be accessible and emotionally supportive. Expected from students, yet still unrecognized by administration.
>
> **Laura. 30s. Professor. #EsportEnthusiast**

To constantly behave in a way that appeases others is tiresome and frustrating. Hochschild[4] identified two components of emotional labor:

1) Surface acting, in which one must manage observable expressions to obey or maintain organizational norms.

2) Deep acting, in which individuals genuinely try to alter their feelings to authentically display positive emotions.

Employees engage in surface acting when they suppress their negative emotions to display anticipated positive expressions, resulting in an emotional dissonance between what they feel and what they display. Employees engage in deep acting when they must adjust to a genuine display of positive emotions as they align with a given situation. Consequently, suppression, or surface acting, has a greater cognitive cost for individuals.[7] It is the surface acting, if not acknowledged, that can be troublesome.

Employees in the service industry are more likely to experience or be exposed to occupational violence while performing their duties, particularly in a modern industrialized society. The highest-risk jobs were found to be "caring jobs" such as teachers, health care providers, police, firefighters, and security workers.[8] These types of scenarios should be acknowledged, addressed, and monitored to ensure the proper training and wellness of individuals involved.

Gendered and Racialized Emotional Labor

In academic literature, the concept of emotional labor has been both gendered[4, 9] and racialized.[10] Most research about emotional labor has emphasized how men's and women's requirements differ.[4, 9] Historically, scholars have revealed women were more likely to display emotions while men suppressed more emotions.[11, 12] Furthermore, women who performed jobs that require emotional labor were significantly more satisfied than men who performed the same job. This work found that with the people-oriented nature of positions of service work, the traditional caretaking roles of women aligned more closely with the work, so women felt authentically involved. Overall, women have a greater tendency to display stronger emotions, compared to men, so they also engage in more emotional regulation to adhere to organizational and societal norms. To further explore all the places invisible work lives in emotional labor, let

54

Our (In)visible Work

us consider Joy, Amber, and Liz's stories.

> As a female professor, compared to my male colleagues, I am expected to be more emotionally aware and available to students. As noted in my evals, students expect me to be a nurturer and to be upbeat in the classroom. Students also expect me to serve as their life coach and then my administration wants me to be the peacekeeper.
>
> **Joy. 40s. Professor. #LatinaBoyMom**

Similar to Joy, Amber was highly aware of her applauded nurturing leadership style; however, she wasn't prepared for how much more emotional labor would be needed after her mother and grandmother's cancer diagnosis.

> Right after my last promotion both my mother and grandmother were diagnosed with cancer. One terminally ill, so as the only child the brunt of the work was on me. After several discussions with my husband and family, I inquired about pausing my promotion and stepping back; however, my supervisor wouldn't listen and doubled down that I'd be fine. Even stating I always manage everything so gracefully. The emotional rollercoaster of being a primary caretaker during a cancer battle while raising young children was something I'd never experienced — all the medical terms are a foreign language, the endless doctor visits, the pain, the sadness, the guilt.

Yet throughout the year, I was still expected to be the team's nurturing

leader at work.

Amber. 40s. Finance Director. #OnlyChildCaretaker

Like Amber, Liz reflects on the emotional toll having to meet

the expectations of being the caring employee while trying to regulate

her own emotions.

I get it. I am in the technology space, but we need to have more care

and concern for people. When I was caring for my dying mother, I

remember how empty my emotional tank was at work and my

supervisor proceeded on like nothing was different. I mean goodness

how am I still one of the only ones in the office caring for people.

Liz. 60s. Technology Specialist. #SingleMom

Twenty years after the genesis of the concept of "emotional

labor," scholars began examining racialized emotional labor.[13, 14]

Historically, it has been a challenge because several institutions still

practice cultural and color blindness, functioning "with the belief that

color or culture make no difference and that all people are the same."[15]

Race had been isolated and outright excluded from public emotional labor

conversations. The perceptions of individuals and institutions regarding

racial identity have a dramatic impact on the experience of minoritized

individuals.[16] Furthermore, with the events of 2020 and calls for action to address racial disparities and inequities in the U.S., greater attention has been on racialized emotional labor.

Two central themes on racialized emotional labor have been constructed. First, colleagues and clients view non-white employees, compared to white employees, as having incongruence with their job until they engage more socially (e.g., additional emotional work), which increases their likelihood of better congruence.[17] In short, the emotional labor of employees of color reduces the racial disparity of their performance judgment. Second, although this racialized emotional labor helps increase role congruences, it also increases their likelihood of experiencing burnout.[18, 19] Although the emotional requirements to address the burden of representation are unlikely to fade, organizations can manage situations differently. For example, if a company is going to ask an individual to be the champion for inclusion efforts, they need to give them resources of time and budget to be able to do so. Allowing for this reduces the likelihood that someone will be overwhelmed with the additional labor.

Spot the Outcomes of Emotional Labor

Emotions must be managed and regulated daily in all aspects of work and life to meet organizational and societal norms. In the workplace, management scholars John Schaubroeck and James Jones[20] revealed emotional labor elicited ill health among employees who identified less, or were less involved, with their jobs. It has been linked to job dissatisfaction, job stress, heart disease, emotional exhaustion, hypertension, memory loss, workplace violence, and burnout, and it has even been found to exacerbate cancer.[21] Emotional exhaustion, one of the most common outcomes of emotional labor, occurs when energy is depleted because of excess emotional demands, particularly by interactions with others[22] or becoming emotionally overextended or exhausted by one's own work.[23] It is clear from research and our interviews that emotional labor cannot be ignored. The strain, work, and stress resulting from this type of labor is hard to see but can have significant negative impacts if left ignored. Joy describes the emotional labor she experiences in the sport industry and acknowledges the inspiration she feels from helping the next generation.

Working in the male-prevalent industry of sports as a Hispanic woman is emotionally exhausting. Every single day — yes, everyday — I am reminded of my gender, my dress, my tone, my age, my emotions, and my place in this space. However, that doesn't stop me; instead, it inspires me to make the space better for the next generation. I am also an educator at heart, so I can always find a teachable moment and provide resources.

Joy. 40s. Professor. #LatinaBoyMom

Mirrors

Practice being self-aware enough to understand when you are

acting versus genuinely feeling an emotion. **Acknowledging the emotional dissonance** you are experiencing is a helpful process. Being present, close your eyes, listen to your heartbeat, and observe your breath. Without judgment be mindful of your thoughts and feelings. **Allow yourself time** to process the emotional experience. If you are engaging in emotional labor, you want to be sure you understand the toll it will take on you. What is your outlet for addressing your own emotions? How do you prioritize self-care? In addition to self-regulating your own emotions, it is imperative to **acknowledge when others are having to exert emotional labor.** Give people the time and create a space to acknowledge and share their own emotional dissonance. Practice active listening.

We realize the importance of our voices only when they are silenced.
Malala Yousafzai, Education Activist

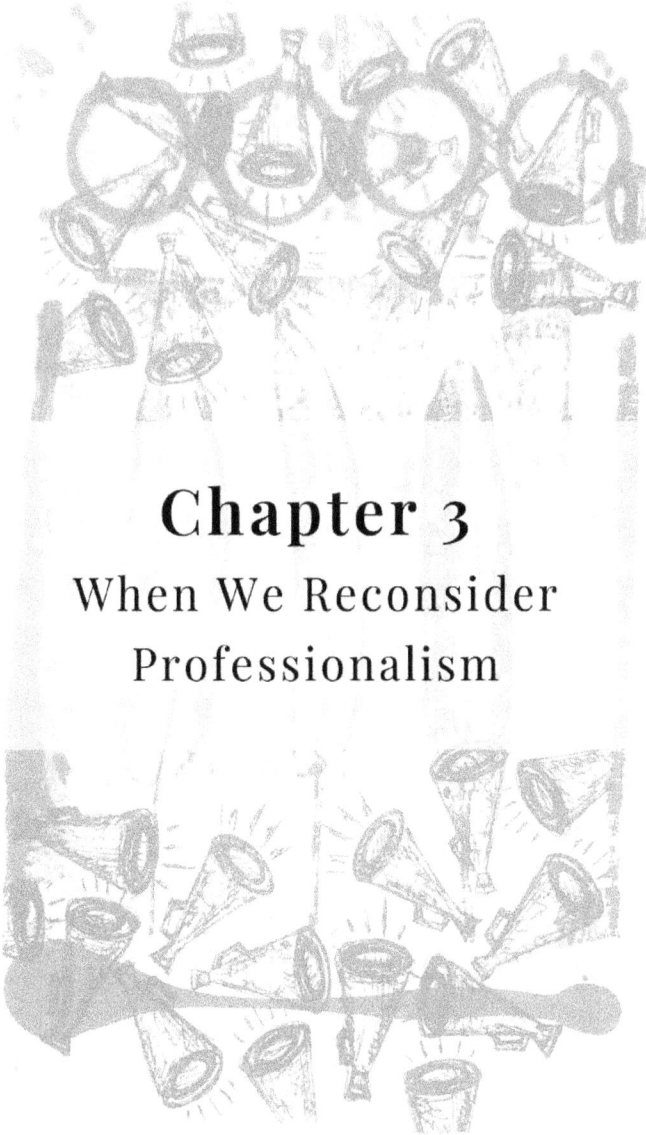

Chapter 3
When We Reconsider Professionalism

3: When We Reconsider Professionalism

Try saying this phrase in three different tones:

- **Say it like you are curious: "What are you doing?"**

- **Say it like you are angry: "What are you doing?"**

- **Say it like you are concerned for the person's well-being: "What are you doing?"**

Is the meaning different if you are speaking to your supervisor or defending a coworker? Is one tone more professional than the other?

The socially constructed nature of professionalism is like a tailored suit. Similar to a suit being custom-made to fit an individual's body, professionalism is custom shaped by society's expectations, norms, and values. Yes, suits can vary by color, fabric, and style, and professionalism varies from one field and organization to another, reflecting the customs and cultures of that organization. Like a well-fitted suit, professionalism appears comfortable and natural when it aligns with societal constructs; however, it can also feel uncomfortable and out of place if it clashes with prevailing norms. Particularly, since the beginning of the pandemic, people have questioned dress codes and embraced athleisure.[1] The importance of understanding the changing styles is important. So, too, is understanding what is "professional." It is the framework for maintaining invisible work in your job. As Khalil transitioned from one industry to another industry, he shared his perspective on professionalism.

Moving from corporate to hospitality and now cannabis, I no longer constantly have to hear others' expectations of me. To be something I'm not, to be toned down, to water down who I am. Professionalism isn't dress, isn't hair color or style. It is treating people with respect no matter what is happening around you. And that can occur with green hair, spiked hair, piercings, and tattoos. Be you, be respectful of others. That's professionalism.

Khalil. 40s. Operations Executive. #GirlDad

Understanding the assumptions around your ideas of professionalism can help identify and bring light to the invisible work that either you or your colleagues are putting in to ensure that they fit in. In examining those assumptions, what things are necessary, and which things are simply done because they have always been done?

In the hustle and bustle of the modern workplace, a significant yet often overlooked aspect of an employee's daily routine is the choice of what to wear to work. Some may dismiss this decision as trivial, but in reality, for those traditionally underrepresented in industries contemplating what outfit to wear takes up valuable time and mental energy and is a form of invisible work that carries profound implications for one's personal well-being and professional success. Adhering to workplace dress codes and norms was felt in Grant's dismemberment of his suits. The required attire for him represented chains of normalcy that stifled who he was in the workplace.

Our (In)visible Work

After 20 years, may I never see a suit again. Oh, how they were a daily reminder of the money I didn't have, the norms I don't want to follow, and the chains I don't want to be locked by. When I left advertising, I burned those things.

Grant. 40s. Entrepreneur. #StorytellingDisruptor

The struggle to appear professional is felt as a struggle for many, as we see in Christine's story about getting ready for work.

Every day that I get ready for work, I just stare at my closet, thinking, "Is this dress professional? Is it too short? Too tight? Too colorful? Are these shoes too high? Too edgy?" Gosh, I am exhausted, and I haven't even left for work yet.

Christine. 40s. Fitness Enthusiast. #SingleMom

Or again, we hear from Khalil and how his attire and tone play a significant role in how he is treated and how he has to actively disarm others in certain situations to ensure he is heard.

If I'm not dressed a certain way, I'm not treated a certain way. As soon as my slacks or business attire come off, I don't get acknowledged or served. So I've learned that my dress, my talk, my tone, my mannerisms, my body language, all of that has to be evaluated and toned down or turned off in certain situations. I've also learned that I over smile to disarm people because naturally they are already

64

defensive interacting with a Black man, so smiling has helped with opening the dialogue and relationship building.

Khalil. 40s. Operations Executive. #GirlDad

The choice of attire also carries implications of identity and personal branding, which we'll discuss in the next chapter. Dress is not the only invisible work of one's appearance. Let's look at Miles' work, thinking about the perceived professionalism of his hairstyle and facial hair.

Until about two years ago, I had to consistently think about my hair and hairstyles. I've had an Afro. I've had dreads. I've had twists, yet just Google "unprofessional hairstyles," and you'll see the majority, if not all, are pictures of Black men. Ah, and then don't even get me started on having to have a clean-shaven face. For seven years, between 2001-2008, I lost track of how many times I was written up by my manager for not meeting the policy of clean shaved — even though I had a doctor's note in my personnel file. Once again, it is such a colonized version of what was and is still considered professional.

Miles. 40s. Finance Executive. #BlackFather

For Grant, Christine, Khalil, and Miles, professionalism looked like organizational culture, not rules, not labels. Yet, Grant was navigating the heterosexual binary gendered corporate world, Christine was blazing a

65

new trail in the male-prevalent industry of sport and entertainment, and Khalil and Miles were code-switching their way through the highly-affluent- White sales industry. For those that need an introduction to code-switching, many underrepresented individuals, generally racial and ethnic, find themselves adept at linguistic agility navigating the complex professional landscape.[2] Born out of necessity, a navigation tool for those who, often unfairly, must traverse between different cultural and professional worlds. In the workplace, employees code-switch to adapt their communication style and tone to meet the expectations and biases of their majority-represented colleagues. Code-switching is a mechanism to mitigate persistent stereotypes and bias, where underrepresented professionals strategically assert themselves, rise through the ranks, and contribute their diverse perspectives to the corporate world. This required code-switching for success is invisible work

In addition to countless stories on dress and appearance, tonality surfaced several times as a taxing labor. Because your voice carries an emotional tone when you are speaking, it reveals aspects of your character, making them critical components of communication. This emotion influences the message that is received. When you are reading, the tone with which you interpret a message also influences the message. This interpretation can have a significant impact on the way the message is received.

Our vocal tone is mostly unconscious, as we have been speaking since we were babies, and even before then, our mother's tone of voice impacted us in the womb. Even at birth, babies have been found to have different accents.[1] To observe the influence of the environment on tone, listen to a radio program from the 1940s or 1950s. You may notice a striking difference to the way people spoke — in part because language is dynamic. It does not remain static over time. For example, on average, women from the mid-20th century spoke softer than women do today. This change has been influenced by the evolving power dynamics between men and women. So if the voice we speak with is influenced by the environment and people around us, one can see how the variability of experiences is extreme.

Communication can be a Catch-22 because we want our own unique voice, yet we are all working in a system with preferred manners of communication and preferred means of communication styles. For example, a perceived wrong tone of voice can affect the messaging and can create misunderstanding and misperceptions in communication, which can lead to confusion, delayed messaging, and a disrespectful interpretation of the message.[3] The concept of tone and the invisible work related to one's use of tone in communication most strongly revealed itself through women's stories. To bring this to life, let us read how one participant vividly recalls a story from 17 years prior when she was told, "You have a tonality problem."

Early on in my career, I was always told I had a tonality problem, so it's something that I've always been hyperconscious of. Having learned a lot about emotional intelligence and the way I phrase things and the way other's receive things, I focus on communicating an effective message without it being abrasive or too assertive.

Elizabeth. 40s. Marketing Executive. #ProudTia

Similar to Elizabeth's experience early in her career, Caroline, who recently started her full-time career journey, is being told to be mindful of her tone.

Gosh, it is exhausting enough to walk onto an all-male sales floor, and yet still be told to be mindful of my tone. Really!

Caroline. 20s. Sales Associate. #DogMom

Like Caroline, Kenzie works in sales, and has for her entire career. As she was reflecting on her 20+ year career, she noted other's discomfort with confidence and directness, masking it as tonality and emotionality.

I'm confident, driven, and direct, always have been, always will be. And for so long folks made it about me, saying I should watch my tone and calm down. I am calm, and I realized it wasn't me. It was them and their discomfort sharing space with a strong, confident, Black woman.

Kenzie. 40s. Sales Executive. #BakingMomma

Our (In)visible Work

These three stories are just a few of the many stories in which women were characterized as having tonality problems simply because society has been socialized and primed to expect a softer, more nurturing tone from a woman.

Societal and Cultural Roles

The difference in tones between women's and men's voices has been well researched. Researchers suggest women's voices are judged more harshly than men's voices. Psychologist Alice Eagly's research on gender and leadership stereotypes[4, 5] reveals that we have been socialized, habituated, and institutionalized to the idea that women should exhibit nurturing characteristics and men should exhibit assertive characteristics as prototypical leaders. So male and female speakers are viewed, heard, and judged differently. Gender-linked social roles and stereotypes greatly sway the expectations of men and women.[4, 5, 6] Historically, women have been expected to be communal, selfless, and socially oriented, while men have been expected to be agentic, self-assertive, and task-oriented.[4, 5] In leadership roles, the prescribed nature of stereotypes has detrimental effects on leadership styles and the evaluation of leaders.[7, 8]

As women's voices can be an octave higher than men's voices, a woman's voice begins with a disadvantage. According to scholars Casey Klofstad and Rindy Anderson,[9] a woman's natural higher pitch can make her be perceived as less certain or submissive in personal or hostile business environments, and as a result lowers her social rank. Conversely, when a deeper voice is heard, it is associated with strength, authority, trust, and higher social rank. A commanding tone is a leadership skill, yet women struggle biologically to create this quality. In addition to pitch, women tend to use more versatile intonation patterns when they speak, placing more emphasis on certain words and speaking about personal topics. According to British linguist Geoff Lindsey, women, mainly young, habitually use vocal fry and upward inflection at the end of sentences (i.e., upspeak), making speaking sound like a constant questioning tonality.[9, 10]

Gender congruence bias develops different perceptions of speakers. Both Elizabeth and Kenzie, female executives, were told they had tonality problems early on and throughout their careers. How much has this tonality challenge cost them? A 2013 study conducted of 792 male CEOs of publicly traded companies revealed deep voices correlated with financial success.[3] While a more masculine style of communication is to give orders such as "We have to do better" or "This is what we need to do," the more feminine style of communication is to persuade, such as "I have an idea for you to consider" or "What do you think about this approach?" because it aligns with gender stereotypes.

Although researchers note these communication styles have been gendered and the perceived male approach is often associated with leadership and strength, there are values to using both approaches to communicate. Many women ascending *the corporate ladder* are told to sound more assertive and direct in their delivery, which scholar Eagly forewarns contradicts the gender expectation for women,[4, 5] so then there is a risk of overcorrection and then being called a "shrill, harsh bitch." So here we go again, having to do (in)visible work to be intentionally aware of the organizational and societal cultures at play so we, women, can make an informed decision about the best vocal approach. Interestingly, in *Give and Take*,[11] author Adam Grant states that using powerless communication reaps rewards by enabling others to put their guard down, which tends to be more influential.

Most people who shared stories about professionalism and tonality were women. Additionally, several mentioned how race and ethnicity played a part in having to self-monitor to meet expectations. Rosa leans into how she has to monitor her passionate Latina side.

> I have to constantly monitor my voice when I'm in the workplace. As a Latina, I am passionate. I talk with my hands. My voice raises when I get excited. Yet often I am told I'm too emotional. I need to calm down my argumentative tone.
>
> **Rosa. 40s. HR Generalist. #LatinaFoodie**

In addition to Kenzie and Rosa, several Black women and men mentioned their constant need to monitor themselves. Malcolm notes changing his tone to be perceived as more likable.

71

I remember one of my professors told me I'm likable because my inviting tone and charismatic smile disarmed folks. Yeah, what a reminder of the additional work I have to do.

Malcolm. 30s. Culture Creator. #EternalOptimist

Whether it is dress, grooming, or tonality, we often do not think about or see the invisible labor that goes into being professional. It takes time and effort to constantly modify how a person expresses themself to meet the norms of an organization, which can interfere with people authentically engaging in the workplace.

Mirrors

At times, we may find our authenticity at odds with our effectiveness because we know the way we communicate in relationships and careers affects how we connect and engage with others. Extending your active listening **try listening to what is being said, not how it is being said.** Communication is a powerful and essential skill, so we must harness our voice and tone to speak with influence and power — yet recognizing there is no silver bullet, just an institutionalized societal expectation. It is time to **question the interpretation and assumptions,** being cognizant of the work and effort that go into clear communication. Everyone's communication style is different, so be mindful of what assumptions you make about their intent based on how you have been socialized to communicate. As colleagues, families, and friends, we can open communication to understand the person and their perspective more.

We can create an inclusive environment that does not judge others simply

based on their tone. By doing this, we start to reduce the amount of

invisible work that goes into trying to monitor, disguise, or otherwise

manipulate one's form of expression.

What I know for sure is that speaking your truth is the most powerful tool we all have.
Oprah Winfrey, Media Mogul

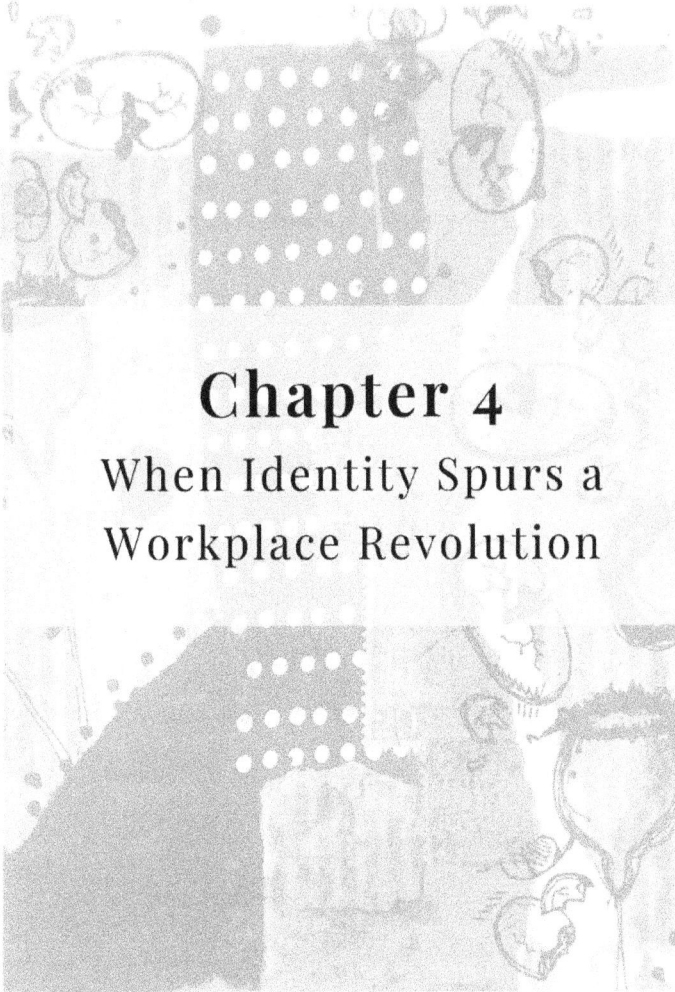

Chapter 4
When Identity Spurs a Workplace Revolution

Our (In)visible Work
4: When Identity Spurs a Workplace Revolution

Have you noticed:

- **A shift in your willingness to share your identity in the workplace?**

- **A shift in your boldness to wear whatever the heck you feel comfortable wearing?**

- **Other people leveraging your identity to engage you as a "volunteer" on a passion project?**

Catalyzed by five generations in the workforce, a pandemic, and a renewed focus on addressing racial inequities, the workplace revolution ushered in an era where employees no longer felt the need to hide their identities at work. As the world grappled with the challenges of the pandemic, conversations around diversity, equity, inclusion, and belonging (DEIB) gained momentum and a workplace revolution emerged. One of the most significant shifts in this revolution was the dismantling of traditional corporate cultures that often-expected employees to conform to a one-size-fits-all mold. Instead, some organizations have recognized the power of embracing employees' diverse backgrounds, experiences, and identities. According to *Harvard Business Review*,[1] diverse teams lead to more innovative problem solving and better decision making. Furthermore, diverse talent is drawn to organizations with workplace flexibility and autonomy.[2]

With the boundaries between personal and professional life

76

blurred, employees found themselves in environments, generally inside their home, where they could be more authentic, no longer having to hide their true selves to fit into rigid office norms. Instead, they could express themselves more casually, whether it was through dress, natural hairstyles, visible tattoos, home office decor, or personal shared spaces revealing aspects of their personality and heritage. For example, Liz shared how in the workplace she'd always hidden her Hispanic heritage in the workplace to gain acceptance and respect in the male-prevalent technology world, but when the pandemic forced her work into her home — her heritage was revealed. She recalls the moment her coworkers realized she spoke another language.

> When we first began working remotely, I remember the first time a coworker heard my son speaking Spanish to me. Their look was priceless when they heard me respond because they had no idea I could speak fluently.
>
> **Liz. 60s. Technology Specialist. #SingleMom**

Another participant had a similar story about hiding a portion of themselves. Trevor hid a part of his identity because of the judgment he constantly felt regarding his sexuality. Trevor began working at an organization six months before the pandemic was declared in March 2020. The organization had a flexible dress code. Some people wore dress shirts with jackets, while others appeared more casual, arriving in jeans and T-shirts. When Trevor went to work, he usually dressed conservatively in

casual pants, a button-up shirt, and a sweater or sport coat — very "beige"
as he would describe. For the next 18 months during the pandemic, he
continued to exhibit the conservative style from the neck up. Then two
years into the new gig, he met with some colleagues outside of normal
business hours for happy hour. A colleague noted that Trevor wore a
fashionable, colorful, "flashy" shirt outside of his "typical" office style.
Trevor shared his experience.

> You should see my closet full of high-fashion attire, but I wouldn't dare
> wear these in the office because my colleagues, both past and present,
> have reacted and made assumptions about my sexuality. Judging me.
> Questioning me. Stereotyping me. And, sadly, once that thought enters
> someone's mind, it puts a shadow over the rest of my work.
>
> **Trevor. 30s. Educator. #AsianFashionista**

As such, Trevor has purposefully altered himself for his coworkers' acceptance and their normative styles, because he had previously
experienced stereotypes about his style and sexuality. Liz and Trevor's
stories are two of several stories that referred to the liberation felt when
remote work became an option. From our research, several people
mentioned the freedom they felt by not having to hide behind
"uncomfortable suits," a "face full of makeup," "a choking necktie," "a
blend-in-sheep style," "dress pants covering my leg tattoo," "appropriate
work hairstyles," or "a straitjacket of corporate cloning," all to portray an

image that meets organizational expectations. Remote work, necessitated by the pandemic, played a pivotal role in identity spurring the workplace revolution. And, yes, although the research is still being collected and analyzed, according to the Bureau of Labor Statistics,[3] in the U.S., employee productivity has risen since the pandemic. Yet, resistant corporate executives are still calling for a full return to in-person 9 to 5 hours. Despite executives' demands, the death of the 9-to-5 gig is happening. Fully remote or hybrid work will continue in the post-pandemic era, especially drawing diverse talent and freedom of expression.

Like Liz and Trevor, have you ever hidden part of your identity for fear of not being accepted? During our inclusive leadership workshops over the last six years, we will often ask participants to consider listing 20 parts of their own identity. We have them think of it in terms of roles they play or values they hold: Are they a sibling, a friend, a child, a spouse, a grandparent, a teacher, an artist, or an engineer? Are they an honest person, an empathetic person, a well-read person, perhaps a sports fan or a lover of baking? Once they have the list, we have them consider what are the most important roles and values to them. Which three are integral to their identity? Then we ask, what if you were not able to show people those parts of your identity? For example, what happens if you had to hide those pieces of who you are from the rest of the world? If they choose the role of being a parent, what would it be like to never talk about raising some of the most significant people in your life? If they selected being a sports fan, how stifling would it be to never talk about sports? Considering this allows individuals to begin to understand the invisible work it takes to be present in a form that is not your authentic self. The effort it takes to watch what you say and how you say it is part of the invisible work.

Each of the roles you play constitutes a piece of who you are as a person, and each of these requires that you behave in certain ways to maintain the role. Consider your interactions with a new supervisor compared to your interactions with a sibling. Although you are the same person in each of the roles, the characteristics of yourself that you reveal to a colleague may be different than the ones you reveal to a loved one. And how do you manage these roles? Or better yet, how do you prioritize each of these roles?

When we look at the different components comprising our identity, we gain insight into the pressures and stress we put on ourselves daily. To understand the strain that invisible work has on all of us, it's important to reflect on how we do not present ourselves the same and it takes energy to show up how we need to show up. For example, if we prioritize being a good spouse, we will need to spend time, energy, and effort to *be* a good spouse. Now, what happens when you hide — hesitantly or willingly — a portion of your identity? Perhaps you do not want people to know you are engaged to be married in fear that they will find out you are a lesbian or question the time you are going to take off or

80

assume once you are a married woman you will want to have children, which some people consider a distraction from work. How do you balance that? Or perhaps it could be not wearing certain clothes, or as Miles and Kevin discussed, having to style their hair in a "professional" way, or perhaps covering up the beauty of henna art after attending an Indian family wedding? Each of these is a way we subscribe to societal and organizational expectations. These expectations vary from workplace to workplace and from community to community. The invisible labor comes in hiding or adjusting who we are.

Our workplace can have an impact on our identity and expression of our identity. Sociologists Susan Halford and Pauline Leonard[4] found that once people had chosen to be part of an organization, that group's norms and values heavily influenced a person's identity as it pertained to being a member. As you work and become part of the organization, your identity becomes influenced by it. This is great for job commitment: if people begin to feel like being an employee at ABC Inc. is part of who they are, they will commit to the organization and its success. An issue can arise if someone begins to abandon their identity to fit the organization. Take, for example, Liz having to mask her Spanish accent in the workplace. If pieces of one's identity become in conflict with one another, this can lead to unnecessary invisible work. It is almost like being an actor performing on stage often to a discriminating audience, and that can be exhausting.

Social Identity

To further understand the performances that we all engage in, let us look at social identity. According to social identity theorists Blake Ashforth and Fred Mael as well as Henri Tajfel and John Turner,[5, 6] the "self" concept comprises personal identity and social identity. Personal identity means peculiar characteristics like traits and abilities, and social identity encompasses salient group classifications like organizational role, religious affiliation, or sport's team fandom. We begin to define groups because of their prototypical characteristics that have either been ascribed to or abstracted from group members. Then, we give meaning to the social environment by identifying ourselves and others in accordance with that environment. Social identification, then, is one's perception of belonging to a classified group: "I am a woman," "I am a member of the Sky Club," or "I am a Tampa Bay Lightning fan."

Speaking of the Lightning, let's talk sports. Think about your own sports fandom or, better yet, think about one of your obnoxious friends who is a die-hard sports fan. That level of fan identification assumes the prototypical characteristics of group membership such that their self-stereotyping begins to depersonalize as they come to see themselves exemplifying the group norms.[7] Your friend begins to develop a sense of who they are, what they value, and how they ought to behave. Josh describes the invisible work of experience social identity conflict in the workplace.

As a sales rep for a National Football League team right after Colin Kaepernick kneeled, I usually talked shop with my clients; however, the heightened racist commentary I had to endure was downright exhausting and painful. All the while, they had no idea they were speaking to a Black man. Coupling that with a lack of internal support, that was a tipping point for me.

Josh. 20s. Lawyer. #BlackExcellence

For those non-sports enthusiasts, or just us casual fans, let's apply this back to our everyday lives. Think about a time you began working for a new company or joined a new association. In that role, you begin to identify with a given group, developing a sense of who they are, what they value, and what their goals and beliefs are. As such, social identity theorists suggest when individuals identify strongly with their role (relatedly as a position, occupation, department, or organization, the role becomes a central component of who they are. [5, 6, 7] The result for an individual is that you begin to conform to that role's expectation. Let's look at Jeremy who works in fan experience, and a portion of his role is to connect with fans. When he is planning and executing themed nights, particularly for historically minoritized groups, he is all in.

> Working for a global brand sport club, I was assisting with a Black history initiative, and leadership wouldn't give us the time or resources. Actually, personally, they knew how important these are to me, and exploited my personal connection even stating, "We know that you'll deliver because you always find a way for pet projects like this."
>
> **Jeremy. 30s. Experience Curator. #QueerBrit**

Even if your social tie to the group is weak, if you feel authentic to the display rules that align with your personal identity values, you feel like "yourself." For example, we are empathetic professors. If our social identity of being a professor is weak, we still feel authentic because our personal identity values are deeply rooted in empathy. One's self-categorization creates a sense of belonging. Generally, people self-categorized or represent themselves at one of three levels of abstraction[7]:

1. the personal level: self as an individual;

2. the collective level: self as a group member;

3. the superordinate level: self as part of a larger group that may include both ingroup and outgroup members.

These levels of abstraction, also known as self-categorization,[7, 8] impact people's motivations, especially those who are considered part of an advantaged group to engage in action for a disadvantaged group.

When self-categorization is at an individual level, it's characterized by the uniqueness an individual feels (their personal identity), guiding emotions, thoughts, and behaviors. Likewise, others see and respond to us in terms of their own personal identities. So, just in case we needed a reminder of the second agreement from the classic, *The Four Agreements*[9] — don't take anything personally. When personal motivations are high, an advantaged group member acts in their own self-interest meeting their own personal needs.

When self-categorization is at a group level, the collective identity guides everyone's thoughts, feelings, and behaviors. Think of the sports notion, "We win together. We lose together." The focus is on the interests, norms, and values of the relevant group, and people respond based on whether they belong (ingroup members) or do not belong (outgroup members).[5] Recalling Josh's story with the NFL team, he no longer felt a part of the ingroup because the goals and interests constrained the advantaged group members to behave and act in ways that did not disrupt the social hierarchy to negatively affect the status of their ingroup.

When self-categorization is at the superordinate group, individuals focus on their shared goals and interests of groups well beyond their local ingroup. One's self-representation is grander than the outgroup-focused motivation. For example, an outgroup-focused advantaged group member will seek to improve the circumstances and status of a disadvantaged group member and genuinely want to see change. A person with a long tenure with the company may actively engage a younger colleague, acting as an ally to ensure the voice of the less tenured person is heard.

Mirrors

Reflecting on spaces where you can be your authentic self, what does the space include? Who is a part of these spaces? Generally, these spaces are built by and with communities of support and trust. When you find yourself hiding pieces of your identity, **be kind to yourself**. Listen to your gut, note what and why you are hiding or adjusting, and then unapologetically enter spaces that encourage and welcome authenticity. Holding up a mirror to yourself, do you offer a space of openness and trust to others? If you or someone you know does reveal their authentic selves to you, **acknowledge the work** it took for them to monitor, manipulate, or even hide it, which is exhausting, at best.

Part 2: WHAT is the Potential and Cost of Invisible Work?

If you do more than your share, you'd better want to: Otherwise, you're paying yourself in a currency recognized nowhere else.
James Richardson, Poet

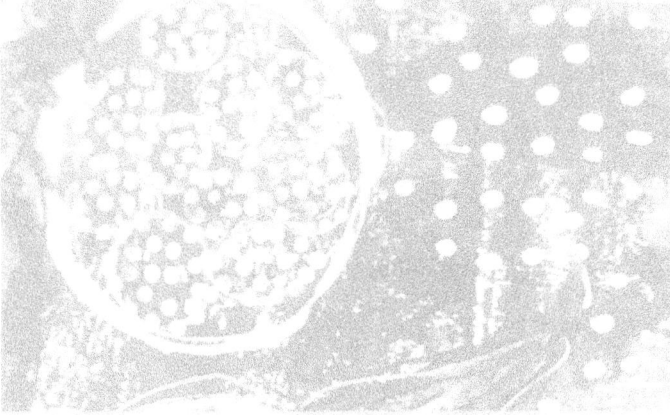

Chapter 5
What Challenges and Opportunities Do We Prioritize?

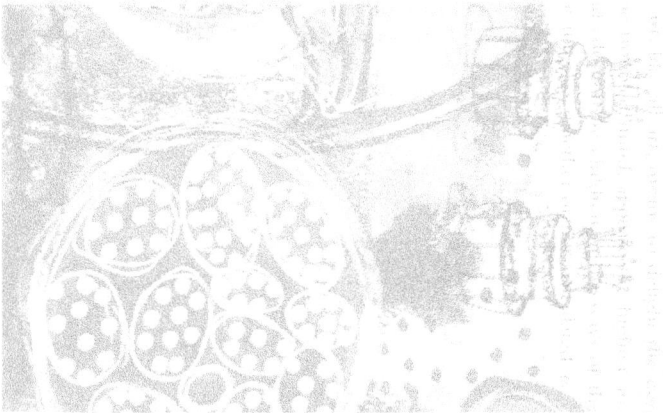

5: What Challenges and Opportunities Do We Prioritize?

When was the last time:

- **You were asked to complete tasks that were not directly related to your job?**

- **Your organization tapped into your strengths to drive results?**

- **You did something fulfilling?**

Many employees, faced with the challenges of navigating a rapidly changing work environment and an uncertain future, found themselves silently reprioritizing and disengaging from their roles. The desire for greater flexibility, a re-evaluation of career priorities, and a quest for work that aligns more closely with personal values have all contributed to the phenomenon popularized as quiet quitting. Or as business scholar Jim Detert appropriately labels it calibrated contributing.[1] While not as overt as quitting signifies, calibrated contributing entails employees assessing what they receive from their work (e.g., compensation, respect, control) versus what they are investing into the work. Essentially, if an employee feels they are giving more than they are getting, they decide to recalibrate their efforts, enacting their views of balance and fairness. This has created a profound transformation in the employment landscape.

One of the most common themes we heard from the stories in our research was how people felt busy, many overwhelmed, yet at the same time felt like their talents, knowledge, and skills were not being utilized. Recently, the phenomenon of being overworked yet underutilized has garnered significant attention in research and professional discourse.[2, 3, 4] This occurs when individuals, despite putting in excessive effort and time at their job, find themselves underutilizing their capabilities and skills, so there is a disconnect between effort and impact. Take executive Elizabeth who has twenty-plus years of advertising experience, yet she was busy educating other executives about the marketing funnel,[5] representing the 16% of minorities on the leadership team serving on the organization's DEI council and experiencing contra-power harassment as one of only three senior women in the organization. Psychologist Katherine Benson[6] first defined contra-power harassment in 1984 explaining that the harasser possesses less formal power (e.g., direct report) than the one being harassed (e.g., supervisor). Contra- power harassment can be exhibited through demands, constant questioning of authority, verbal bullying, eye rolling, publicly arguing, and constantly interrupting. Laura, a college professor, relives the constant student demands and questions.

> Unlike my male colleague, students will challenge me more when it comes to class discussions, grades, and decisions I've made. One email challenging me turns into five emails back and forth and then meeting with my Chair [supervisor]. Yet, discuss it with my male counterparts, and they don't even get asked.
>
> **Laura. 30s. Professor. #EsportEnthusiast**

Our (In)visible Work

Even outside of the classroom, scholars have revealed that contra-power harassment of female executives interrupts their careers, commitment, and productivity, while also increasing their tendency to quit.[7] Facing these challenges and opportunities of the work, Elizabeth concisely stated:

I feel like I'm overworked and underutilized.

Elizabeth. 40s. Marketing Executive. #ProudTia

Elizabeth succinctly stated what many lengthy stories were describing. People found themselves in roles that took time and energy away from their job duties, yet went unrecognized as an asset. Rosa notes how her bilingual skills were overworked and underutilized.

Because I speak two languages, I am constantly asked to come translate even if it isn't related to my job duties. There could be a meeting going on and I'm pulled from my work to come help. I am also regularly asked to translate briefing documents.

Rosa. 40s. HR Generalist. #LatinaFoodie

Rosa's story grew deeper as she explained after a full workday she was up all night translating the briefing for new clients in Mexico. Both Elizabeth and Rosa felt that they did not have the option to decline the additional service work without retribution. For others, the feeling of being overworked was captured by stories on being the token individual

92

who was assigned to "mentor every similar looking colleague who joined the firm," or constantly being asked to "organize the happy hours because you like doing that," or being directed to "take the notes" as you recognize you are the token woman in the room, yet you have a Ph.D. and are not the most junior employee in the room, or as Danielle notes after a decade working with the same people: Why doesn't anyone else remember when it is our office manager's birthday?

Why is it that every year for over a decade now, I am the one always getting the birthday cards, getting them signed, and collecting the money?

Danielle. 50s. Director. #ClimbingEnthusiast

In these scenarios, the invisible work is taking up their time and energy, yet isn't related to assigned job duties or annual performance reviews. And instead of acknowledging the contribution of such roles by providing the time and space or alleviating responsibilities elsewhere, individuals find themselves recalibrating their contributions, being resentful, or being overworked. Taking the focus away from their tasks without recognition can lead to them working beyond the hours required of their position and experiencing stress of not being able to perform at the same level as colleagues who aren't expected to engage in these types of activities.

The issue of not recognizing the work of individuals who

93

perform the indirect activities for an organization can be explained through organizational justice theory. Scholar Jerald Greenberg[8] developed the theory in 1987, extending literature on equity in the workplace. The theory looked at how individuals perceive the behaviors of other people. The concept has since developed to consider four types of justice in the workplace: procedural, distributive, informational, and interactional.

Procedural justice, which looks at the steps applied to see if they are administered equally each time. For example, if there are training opportunities for individuals at an organization, does everyone know how to apply for them? In Janice's last position, she experienced unfair procedures, which enticed her to start her own business.

> At my last position, I touched every part of the business, was a people pleaser, always burning out to get the job done behind the scenes, so when I got passed over for a promotion again, I no longer could bear to hear procedural excuses from my boss.
>
> **Janice. 30s. Business Owner. #AvidReader**

Next, there is distributive justice, which focuses on the disbursement of rewards and resources within an organization. Are rewards and resources fairly handed out throughout the organization? If people are being asked to work on tasks unrelated to their performance goals, and their remuneration is based on the same goals as others, there is a sense of unfairness that arises. For example, both Rosa and her

94

counterpart have the same job tasks except Rosa is also expected to be the office translator. When the obligation to translate took away from Rosa's assigned tasks related to her role and she was given no grace on meeting deadlines, yet was being held to the same standards as the people that do not have to spend time translating documents, she began feeling a sense of inequity.

Informational justice looks at how information is communicated within the workplace. It is not only about having information, it also includes having access to information. And if people do not have access to the data, is there a logical reason? For example, if there is a position that will be opening for people to apply for, but only a few people are informed about the details, this lack of access to information causes a feeling of injustice. The final form of organizational justice is interactional justice, which discusses the relationships people have with others in their workplace. For example, if a colleague is being asked to head up an Employee Resource Group (ERG) involving senior managers, then their counterpart might feel as though the colleague is gaining access to beneficial people and information, they themselves do not have.

Looking at these issues through organizational justice theory, it is important to see that the ramifications are not only that you have certain employees with too much on their plate to contribute their knowledge and talents, but you can also have an environment where people don't feel as though they're being treated fairly. See Nola's realization of her unfair treatment.

> When I was an early-career professor, I had created new courses, new shells for online courses, and there was a faculty member quite a bit older than me. Here I am excited and energized about building new course content, new online shells, and new syllabi. Not even halfway into the semester, this faculty member was raising his hand and asking to teach my classes and had the audacity to ask if he could get copies of my work. I remember feeling really frustrated because on one hand I wanted to be a team player and share, you know, but on the other hand he didn't want to do the work and was taking advantage of me. I was the youngest person in the department. It was expected that I would do all of these new things and build out all of these new things and then hand them over to the more senior members of the department for the subsequent semester.
>
> **Nola. 40s. Administration Executive. #FierceMomma**

Procedurally, no one offered to help Nola by sharing their existing course content when she first started. If this was the norm, why wasn't she made aware or offered assistance by her colleagues? Similar to the unfair treatment Nola experienced, even as a program leader Danielle is often excluded from gaining access to pertinent resources that others in similar roles are being given access to more freely.

I am constantly advocating for our students, our program, our partners, our faculty. However, sometimes there are rooms I'm not in, yet my male counterparts have access.

Danielle. 50s. Director. #ClimbingEnthusiast

Access discrimination is not the only issue. There is often an unequal distribution of tasks, especially the ones that mean little in the evaluation process. For example, from a distributive justice standpoint, in Laura's role as a college professor she was experiencing being overworked with service expectations. This burden, which was not felt by all colleagues, leaves someone like Laura at a disadvantage when her performance is evaluated.

It is funny when you sit on these university committees. Data reveals that the majority of faculty in higher education are a higher proportion of men, yet somehow whenever I enter the room for a committee meeting, which counts as service to the institution, it's like all women in the room. And we know service doesn't get rewarded in higher education.

Laura. 30s. Professor. #EsportEnthusiast

When people enter the workplace, they do so with years of education, experience, and knowledge. They apply and go into that position with the hope of using all they've acquired and can become disengaged when they realize the talents, skills, and knowledge they can offer are not being used at all. Similar to Elizabeth, the word underutilized was described by many in our research as "bored," "uninterested," or even "mindless" with their work. Perhaps there wasn't enough work, so they felt "pigeon-hold" or even "stalled," and it was demoralizing and frustrating. When you feel overworked and underutilized, your mind, body, and spirit often are stressed and overwhelmed, causing even the simplest task to seem more challenging.

Wellness has become a salient endeavor for research and practice.[8, 9, 10] Organizations offer programs on everything from managing your time, practicing mindfulness, to participating in yoga classes as a means to encourage wellness and release stress for employees. Although these are extremely important for any individual in an organization, we challenge you to think of the root cause of the stress to begin with. As Jeremy noted he was "boredly drowning" in the workplace.

> This job is destroying my mental and physical well-being, and I'm not even in my mid-30s yet. But here I am, juggling, doing my darndest, and I am boredly drowning. I have one employee out on sick leave, another who barely wants to come to work, and another who refuses to use email, but they won't retire, either. So here I am doing mindless tasks, yet too busy putting out fires that I can't take personal time or even see the rain clouds headed my way.
>
> **Jeremy. 30s. Experience Curator. #QueerBrit**

Jeremy had a sense of constantly putting out fires instead of having the time and resources needed to perform effectively in the position for which they were hired. Jeremy is an example of shifting from organizational wellness to organizational resilience.[11] Having resilience acknowledges the inevitable adversity each person encounters in their life and work, allowing for tension and flexibility between all facets of life.

Feeling overworked and underutilized, however, doesn't only surface as an issue in the workplace, but in the navigation of home and community. For example, hosting holiday events Nola sarcastically reasons with herself about the lack of acknowledgement of the work it takes.

> Why is it every Thanksgiving I'm not asked anymore, it is just expected that I host. Some folks still walk in 15 minutes before and ask how they can help. Where were you days ago — when we were planning, checking on dietary restrictions, shopping, prepping the food, cleaning the house, setting the space and table?
>
> **Nola. 40s. Administration Executive. #FierceMomma**

The challenges of negotiating work, family, and life have drawn increasing attention in academic research, public debate, and policy analysis. Over the past 30 years in the U.S., the average age of marrying has increased, the age for birthing one's first child has increased, and the number of children per household has declined.[12, 13] Single women spend less time doing housework compared to married women, and those without children do less housework, on average, compared to those who are parents. These demographic trends provide people more leisure time without reducing their time on the job.[14]

Mirrors

The juxtaposition of being overworked, yet feeling underutilized is a byproduct of invisible work. Constantly doing invisible work secretly maintains the status quo and limits one's full potential. The invisible work unknowingly steals time, energy, and bandwidth. Hold up a mirror to **reassess job responsibilities, integrate data,** and **benchmark workload** for yourself and your direct reports. To **reassess job responsibilities**, identify what tasks are really required to successfully fulfill the position. Assess what work is regularly completed versus what is being evaluated. Is there alignment in work distribution? To identify any misalignment, journal for a month to see exactly where the hours are spent. One way to bring light to work is to **integrate data.** The data could include hours spent, impact of work, performance metrics — let the data do the storytelling. Having an audit will also allow one to **benchmark workload.** To identify if the work is outside of the original job description requirements or if the workload is manageable. Being overworked is not an inevitable state. Ensure time and priority management of your workload is realistic.

Our (In)visible Work

Only by learning to live in harmony with your contradictions can you keep it all afloat.
Audre Lorde, Poet

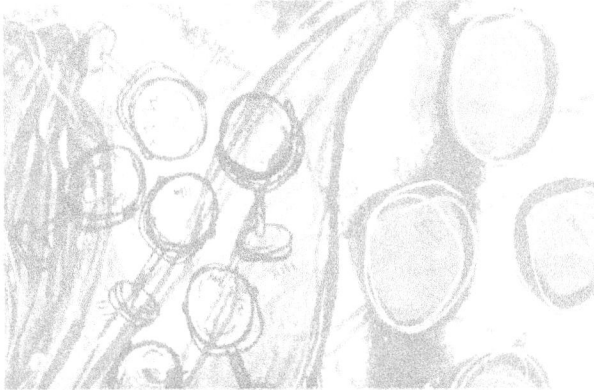

Chapter 6

What Is Intersectional Perspective — and What Does It Unlock?

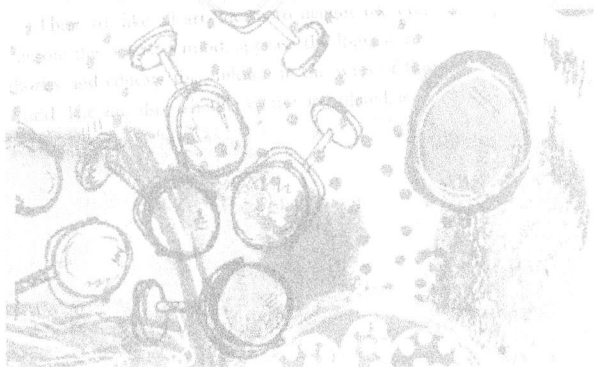

6: What Is Intersectional Perspective — and What Does It Unlock?

Are you rich or poor?

Are you a friend or a family member?

Are you a parent or a child?

Are you Black or White?

Or are you all of the above?

Your lived experience is like no other. Your identity or identities are unique. Thus, we cannot assume others have the same lived experiences as we do. While there may be a dominant noticeable identity, due to how society categorizes class, gender, race, and abilities, an interaction may exist. The overlap of one's social identities is what is known as intersectionality. Incorporating an intersectional perspective in our book is important to broaden perspectives. As noted in the Preface, we refrain from using "women" as code for "white women" and "men" as universal for "white men," which would erroneously ignore other social identities. Understanding intersectionality requires a unique way of thinking because of the additive way identities operate, not stand alone.

Grounded in Black feminist theory, Columbia law professor Kimberlé Crenshaw's groundbreaking research[1] challenged traditional studies of women to consider how sociopolitical inequities shape other identities women hold, such as class, sexual orientation, and race. Today, 30 years post-inception, Crenshaw[2] notes intersectionality is "basically a lens, a prism, for seeing the way in which various forms of inequality often operate together and exacerbate each other." Historically, society has focused on racial inequality as if it were separate from inequalities based on one's class, sexuality, immigrant status, religion, language, neurodiversity, parental status, gender, age, or ableism. This focus misses the fact that people are subject to multiple inequalities and experiences that are more than the sum of their parts.

Take the interaction of income and gender inequality. In 2007, sociology scholars Shelley Correll, Stephen Benard, and In Paik[3] revealed mothers, compared to fathers, suffer a substantial wage penalty. More recently, Mom Project,[4] a career-resource platform for working mothers, and Moms First,[5] a nonprofit, revealed on average, women do two-thirds of the caregiving at home, and they lose 4% of their income for every child, while men gain 6% for every child. Popularized to be the "motherhood penalty," research reveals women still get paid less for the same work. Multiply that over a lifetime of circumstances if a woman stayed home to child-rear and/or experienced a divorce, and the impact on the earning potential of women, compared to men, is more profound. Take Liz's story as a single mother in the male-prevalent technology industry, where she has consistently wondered why she is significantly underpaid.

> I have spent too much time thinking and fighting for equal pay. Contemplating the reasons why and gathering data to support. I have spent too much time thinking and fighting for equal pay. Contemplating the reasons why and gathering data to support.

> Is it because I am a woman? Is it because I am in a male- dominated
>
> field? Is it because I am Latina? Is it because I am a parent?
>
> **Liz. 60s. Technology Specialist. #SingleMom**

Even before having the opportunity to become a mother, researchers have long informed society that men are hired based on potential and women are hired based on past performance.[6] Particularly, for leadership positions, women are hired because of leadership performance, and men are hired because of leadership potential. While women represent 48% of the global working population, women around the world only represent 37% of managerial positions.[7, 8] At the highest level of leadership (e.g., C-suite), that female representation drops to 28%.[7, 8] Gender bias in hiring and promoting has been a salient research endeavor for decades, moving from processes to causes. In our research, the intersectionality of parental status rose to the surface. Too often, women interviewing in their "prime childbearing years," in reality or perception, recall hearing inappropriate questions during the hiring or promotion process:

- Can you still do this work after having a child?
- Will you be able to handle the work after having a child?
- Will you return to work?
- Will parenthood interfere with your performance?
- How will you balance work and life?

Our (In)visible Work
Stop asking about work-life "balance" — there is no such thing.

Since our economy has been recovering from the pandemic, according to UN Women[9] and the Society for Human Resource Management,[10] women are being left behind in the workforce. There is no going back to normal. Normal was never working in the first place, so let it be known women can be mothers *and* executives, mothers *and* professors, mothers *and* doctors, mothers *and* referees, mothers *and* athletes, mothers *and* "you name any profession or role." And according to Joy, it isn't an either-or question.

In 2017, I interviewed for my third job in higher education. After 14 years of experience, this wasn't my first, second, or third rodeo when it came to interviewing. Throughout the course of my career, I'd taken stops in the collegiate coaching arena and the private sector before earning my doctorate at the ripe age of 31. I started having kids somewhere in there, too. At the time of this interview, I was 37 years old and three kids deep, with a productive trail of accomplishments and a healthy line of future research. I can still see the look of surprise on the interviewer's face when he looked back and forth between my resume, face, and a slide depicting my value for family (that I intentionally included). I knew I had convinced him I'd be a productive scholar because I already had *been* so productive: A productive educator, a productive mother, and, yes, a productive scholar. I got the job. To this day, don't dare question my ability to raise children, publish, teach, *and* serve others. It isn't an either-or question.

Joy. 40s. Professor. #LatinaBoyMom

Crenshaw urged us to be attuned to the intersectional experiences of identities to acknowledge key assertions of intersectionality. For women, in general, many of us have a shared experience of workplace gender discrimination; however, not all have experienced gender-race discrimination or gender-race-sexual orientation discrimination. Yet, Black women and Black Queer women have these double- or triple-marginalized identities.[1, 11] One of the biggest stories in sports in 2022 was Brittney Griner's detention abroad. The gender pay gap led Brittney to play in Russia and become a political pawn. Media constantly discussed her intersecting identities as a professional athlete, a Black woman, a lesbian, and a U.S. citizen.[11, 12, 13]

Although intersectionality is rooted in Black feminist research, it transcends an individual's lived experience within social systems.[11, 13] For example, social systems have unique power dynamics that manifest what has always existed, whether by design, institutionalization, or force. Intersectionality is not a zero-sum game, so do not make the mistake of trying to decipher which identity group is the most oppressed in comparison to others.[11, 13] If you do, you will miss the complexity and limit the utility of intersectionality. If you just listen, whether to yourself or others, you can hear the intersectionality surface. See Nola's and Josh's stories.

You don't know, really, which demographic feature is at play. Once, I was the only Black faculty member in a department, but I was also the youngest faculty member in the department, and I think there were only two women. It was a small department, the other woman was the Department Chair, so she was older and more experienced, but I don't know exactly what it was — was it my view, was it my race, was it my gender? In my gut sense, I feel like it was age, because I was substantially younger than everybody else and was always told, "Oh my gosh, you have so much energy" and "You're doing so much." And so, I just think that it was assumed that I would continue doing so much.

Nola. 40s. Administration Executive. #FierceMomma

Similarly, Josh reflects on his intersecting identities.

Historically, I lean into which demographic feature is visible; however, as my career progresses many assumptions are made about my age, education, and social status. When I'm told, "You look too young to be a...," I have to explicitly weave my experience and educational journey into my story.

Josh. 20s. Lawyer. #BlackExcellence

Unpacking the intersectionality of race, gender, and education,

109

Our (In)visible Work

Josh has experienced several challenges as one of only two Black men at a law firm; however, as a male lawyer from one of the top law schools in the country, he was also afforded access to high-resourced networks. Educational background can intersect to create disparities and parity in the workplace. Jeremy recalls navigating his intersecting identities of sexuality, education, and citizenship.

> Reflecting on my time in the States, I was naive to believe the more progressive U.S. laws and higher education options would afford me greater opportunities; however, the social and political height of 2016 made it disadvantageous for me.
>
> **Jeremy. 30s. Experience Curator. #QueerBrit**

Another interaction, especially relevant to educational sectors is the interaction of neurodiversity, gender, class, and education. These four can intersect to create disparities in the workplace. With dyslexia, for example, one story showed us the many challenges a person with this neurodevelopment condition faces growing up in a public school where the stereotypes and stigma of being sent to a closet to study as a "special student" led to unnecessary struggles. See Jacqueline's story and how the shame from early treatment inhibited her abilities as an academic.

As a professor, I am still hesitant to let people help me with my writing. I get embarrassed to share because of my dyslexia. It is something I was taught to keep quiet. I remember the first time I had to get help for my writing because my tests did not match my IQ. I was taken out of class and walked down to a room the size of a school broom closet to work on memorizing my words, so I wouldn't get them wrong. I was made to feel like I was just not working hard enough. And unlike today my family didn't have the means for additional resources.

Jacqueline. 40s. Academic. #AlwaysLearning

No matter the identity or industry, there are examples everywhere. Think of your own experiences, whether personally experienced or observed. Go back to chapter 4 and look at the identity exercise we discussed. List 10 of your identities and roles. How have those identities intersected throughout your lived experience, particularly surfacing as invisible work?

Understanding intersectionality is like peering through a kaleidoscope, revealing the intricate patterns of individual identities and experiences. It unlocks a world of empathy and insight, where we grasp the profound impact of intersecting aspects of identity on a person's life journey. Intersectionality is the key to opening the way for social change and dismantling oppressive structures, as it unveils hidden biases and allows us to design equitable policies and practices. With this knowledge, we can unlock the door to a more inclusive and just society, where the diverse stories of individuals are seen, heard, and ideally valued.

Mirrors

Everyone wears multiple hats, experiences multiple roles, and adheres to multiple identities. If we try to dissect one identity, we miss the **power and complexity** of us as human beings. As you've held up that mirror to your 10 identities and roles, take the time to reflect on how they interact, and where they interact most. Then be sure to hold up a mirror for someone else — your friend, your partner, your colleague, and your supervisor. Ask them to explain the complex person they see. And let them explain what hasn't been seen, heard, or valued.

Part 3: WHO Can Reshape the Invisible Economy?

No one can make you feel inferior without your consent.
Eleanor Roosevelt, Former First Lady

Chapter 7
Who Broke It — and Why They're Best Positioned to Fix It

7: Who Broke It — and Why They're Best Positioned to Fix It

Profits are falling. Who takes the risky project?

Employees are disengaged. Who implements the well-being initiatives?

Your house looks like a hurricane hit it. Who cleans it?

The retirement party is tomorrow, and we don't have a cake. Who makes or buys it?

Who are we going to call? Nope, not the Ghostbusters.

We're calling women, particularly Black women. Yet, they are not your savior. They are not your Tylenol or your cure for foolishness. And yet, women are consistently called upon to help when profits fall, customers are outraged, employees are disengaged, a house is a disaster, or a last-minute party needs cake. Throughout history there has been an unhealthy obsession positioning certain individuals as only worthy to serve, to save, or to solve when societal and operational ills call. See Patti's Black woman savior example.

> For over five decades, this organization has never authentically targeted the Black and Latina community, and all of the sudden they hire me and expect me to fix it within months.
>
> **Patti. 30s. Business Developer. #SingleWorldTraveler**

Like Patti, Danielle was expected to fix the lack of representation.

116

In 2015, I was presenting a research project to a newly created Advisory Board with my dear friend and colleague. Thankfully, when we walked into the room, the two of us increased the percentage of women to 15%. (Sadly, this is an everyday occurrence in sports and entertainment: walking into a room or entering a Zoom conference with, at most, few to no women.) I made eye contact with the lone woman at the table. She looked up, smiled, and gave us a universal head nod that read as, "Kill it." Let it be known we did. When I asked the executive director, "Where were all the women?" He tried to excuse his way around the topic until finally asking, "Can you two help us fix it? You'd be a great resource and mentor."

Danielle. 50s. Director. #ClimbingEnthusiast

Highly regarded in their industries, Patti and Danielle were expected to resolve the long- standing misrepresentation and serve as mentors for the respective underrepresented individuals. Yes, these organizations were signaling a change was coming; however, Patti was brand new to the organization and Danielle wasn't even on the Board. Yet, both were expected to fix and then develop it.

Women are earning degrees and entering the workforce at the highest rates in history; however, when it comes to being promoted into leadership positions, the number remains stagnant and even declines in some industries. Between 2018 and 2019, according to McKinsey &

Our (In)visible Work

Company[1] for every 100 men promoted to management positions, only 68 Latina women were promoted and 58 Black women. The 50-year-old adage "Think manager — think male" is alive and well today.[2, 3] Scholars Alice Eagly and Wendy Wood's[4] research revealed women are perceived to possess more communal traits, such as being caring, nurturing, and cooperative, whereas men are perceived to exhibit more agentic traits, such as being dominant, assertive, and independent. In turn, these masculine stereotypes are more closely aligned with leadership stereotypes, leading men to generally be seen as a better fit for leadership positions.

Social scientists Michelle Ryan and Alex Haslam[5] demonstrated people have a stronger belief in a female candidate's ability to signal change is coming, but not her ability to be effective in the leadership position. Those who have broken through glass walls[5] or glass ceilings may be more likely to find themselves on a glass cliff — finally promoted into a leadership position, usually in times of crisis, duress, or a recession, that is seen as relatively risky or precarious compared to their White male counterparts.[6, 7, 8]

Scholars Michelle Ryan and Alexander Haslam coined the term "glass cliff" in 2005 when they re-analyzed data from a popular article in *The Times* that wrongfully weaponized women's leadership as wreaking "havoc on companies' performance."[5] Ryan and Haslam[5] revealed these women were appointed to boards after companies experienced sustained patterns of poor share price performance;

however, they were the "fall guy" and not quick saviors. After years of turmoil Elizabeth recalls being hired as the head of brand, and within a year she was informed she did not act quickly enough.

> Essentially, when I was hired, I walked into a burning building, was highly encouraged to let some people go (that was gasoline being poured onto the fire), and then I had to rebuild the foundation. Yet, they say I didn't do it fast enough.
>
> **Elizabeth. 40s. Marketing Executive. #ProudTia**

In times of crisis, evidence suggests, organizations strategically shy away from standard leadership practices and appoint a non-prototypical leader to signal to stakeholders that they are undertaking a change. When dealing with a crisis, the association between masculinity and leadership reverses, and the stereotypical feminine communal characteristics (e.g., nurturing, helpful) become vital traits for leaders, describing what scholars refer to as "Think crisis — think female" association.[7] Particularly in countries with greater gender equality, women are more likely to be selected over men as leaders in times of crisis. Furthermore, researchers[9, 10] revealed gendered stereotypes interact with ethnic stereotypes. For example, Asian stereotypes compared to White stereotypes are considered more feminine, while Black stereotypes are considered more masculine.[9, 10] In 2019, researchers discovered an extension to the gender association of "Think crisis — think female" for East Asian Americans.[11] Rosa shares how she felt exploited as a woman of color to nurture the organization's diversity efforts.

> After the murder of George Floyd, our organization created a DEI Council. Of course, I raised my hand; however, after two years serving, making an impact even without dedicated resources or respect for our contributions from executives, I had enough. The C-suite continuously expected me to kindly deliver the realities to the Council that there were no resources.
>
> **Rosa. 40s. HR Generalist. #LatinaFoodie**

Evidence of the glass cliff has extended to racially and ethnically underrepresented individuals.[9, 10, 11, 12] In June 2020, Fortune reported five Black CEOs, which was a scant 1%. Over a 15-year period, professors Alison Cook and Christine Glass[12] analyzed Fortune 500 companies and revealed members of occupational minorities (like women and Black men) were more likely to be promoted to a CEO position after the organization experienced a decline in performance. Khalil reflects on his 15 years of leadership opportunities, noting that most, if not all, were to fix dysfunctional scenarios throughout his career.

> I find myself in these leadership positions — the repair mode of fixing things that other people can't fix. Or they recruit people like me, people of color and women, to fix it. We are put in dysfunctional scenarios to save the day. It is an uphill battle that no matter what you do, you'll never really feel as though you're making progress.

However, you're laying enough of a foundation for someone else to learn later that you did make it better, you fixed the foundation. Instead of getting the legacy positions or inheriting a successful team to come in and fine tune the bells and whistles. We don't tend to be put in those same positions; we get the fix-it opportunities.

Khalil. 40s. Operations Executive. #GirlDad

Echoing Khalil's sentiments throughout his career, Miles notes how often he is recruiting for precarious leadership positions.

I've lost count of how many recruiting calls I get for CEO roles at organizations that are in financial disarray.

Miles. 40s. Finance Executive. #BlackFather

Like Miles' experience on the business side of sport, a 30-year review of the U.S. collegiate men's basketball coaches led Cook and Glass[12] to uncover a glass cliff for ethnic minority coaches. They were more likely to be appointed head coach if the team had a history of losses the year prior.

These glass cliffs have transcended demographics and are contextualized by industry and geography. From politics, law, and sports to education, glass cliffs have no geographic boundaries, as several researchers have found prevalence in Canada, Germany, Switzerland, Turkey, the U.S., the United Kingdom, and Canada. [13, 14, 15, 16] In 2020,

Our (In)visible Work

psychologists Thekla Morgenroth, Teri Kirby, Michelle Ryan, and Antonia Sudkamper conducted a meta-analysis of 74 existing studies on the glass cliff and found mixed evidence.[17] Noting that while there was no universal glass cliff situation, there was a variety of reasoning and sensemaking of it. Although everyone may not occupy precarious leadership positions, the evidence supports women and ethnic minorities are overrepresented in glass cliff positions.

Being in a leadership position with authority and power to make decisions is imperative to bringing visibility to the invisible. Although having access and connections to higher-level organizational members increases your access to influence, information, and resources,[8, 17] historically, underrepresented individuals have been less likely to have diverse or high-status networks.[18, 19, 20] Coupled with the fact that individuals prefer functioning in homogenous groups,[19, 20] for centuries having access to the John CEOs of the world created advantages mainly for those that looked most like John.[21] In 2015, the New York Times[21] ran a story about how more men named John were running big companies compared to the total number of women CEOs. According to Bloomberg,[22] in 2018, for the first time, female CEOs outnumbered any single male name among the S&P 500 CEOs; however, one year later, in 2019, women CEOs tied with men CEOs named James. That was true until the pandemic year and beyond. Also diminishing the preponderance of John S&P 500 CEOs has been the rise of unique first name CEOs growing from 133 in 2015 to 186 in 2023.[21, 22]

Predicated upon the resources you have access to within your network, and the exclusive property of the elites who protect it to continue securing their positions, those that designed or reinforced the current system are the ones that must work to fix it. Now is the time for *moral ownership,* leveraging your social capital (e.g., network) to foster trust, dictate resource flow, provide access to positions, and risk your reputation to enhance their reputation. Moral ownership occurs when individuals or entities responsible for a predicament bear a heightened sense of responsibility and are motivated to resolve it.[23]

Ideally, at this juncture in the book, you can identify invisible work, so now, it is time to acknowledge the system and our role within the system that helped create the invisible. If you are the one upholding the system or have intimate involvement, then you possess an advantage to develop targeted solutions. Researchers support the notion that those proximate to a problem showcase a deeper comprehension of its complexities, thereby demonstrating a unique vantage point from which to engineer effective interventions. To make lasting change and encourage accountability within systems, entrusting the task of rectification to those accountable for a problem is a viable strategic approach to increase a vested interest in achieving sustainable resolutions.

Making Changes

Many of the stories we heard about being overlooked, overworked, and underutilized kept referring to completing tasks that were unrelated to their position or areas of expertise — all because others made assumptions about parts of their personal identities. When people were asked to complete a task like arranging social events, ordering food for events, note taking, mentoring, counseling, or spearheading inclusion initiatives within the organization there was always a reference point to one's identity or "passion project." So, if we want to make it easier on our employees, do we need to alleviate some of these tasks? The answer we hope you're saying to yourself is *no*. That is right, read that again: The answer is *no*. As organizations are becoming more aware of the importance of organizational culture, there is a need for employees to be doing a lot of these activities, **keeping information flowing, courageously helping individuals stay committed and motivated.** The individuals that find themselves doing these tasks are concerned with the well-being and sense of community within an organization. As leadership scholar Amy C. Edmondson highlights in *The Fearless Organization* workplaces flourish when people openly share concerns, mistakes, half-baked ideas, and questions.[24]

Building a culture that people want to be a part of does not happen without people taking on the responsibility to ensure that the values of the organization are evident in the day-to-day operations of the organization. Engaged employees are more satisfied employees, which isn't only good for the bottom line, but also for the people you are working with as well.

Our (In)visible Work

If we truly want to value engagement and the people in our organization, we need to find ways to infuse these tasks into the job descriptions of the individuals who are completing the tasks. What needs to happen is a recognition of this work and its value toward the overall goal of the organization.

One way to do this is to ensure there is a well-crafted and agile job description. The job description is the reference point for one's work duties, and most human resources professionals will refer to it when someone is being hired or disciplined. However, in some industries, rarely is it something that's reviewed and updated on a regular basis. Therefore, individuals may see that organizations have the "tasks as assigned" clause — because when someone leaves a position, especially if they've held that role for a while, the job description for a new hire isn't reflective of the actual tasks performed by the individual who had the position. Remember Rosa's experience translating. Although she fluently spoke Spanish, it was not part of her job description, so what will happen with her replacement one day?

In fact, if an organization wants to stay dynamic and agile, they need to include such verbiage in the job description to account for the changing workplace, and the changing workforce. When we're developing a job description, it is extremely difficult to be able to identify all of the tasks someone will need to complete. It is a buffer of sorts. But what happens when the same person is asked time and time again because of a skill set or a passion they may have? Some people keep being asked to do these invisible tasks that their other counterparts in the organization are not asked to do, and that becomes problematic.

Another way we can address undervaluing tasks is to check our biases and misperceptions. In the newly released book *Glass Walls*,[5] social scientists Amy Diehl and Leanne M. Dzubinski provide a roadmap for individuals, management, and allies to shatter gender barriers that surround women. As our participants reflected on why they were expected to do these tasks, some had jarring recollections where colleagues said: "You are a woman. You like that stuff," "You are one of them, so you would understand that struggle more," and "It comes more naturally to you." Now in some of these cases, these comments might have held some truth. Maybe counseling people *does* come more easily to some colleagues than others, but this does not mean that if the person willingly agrees to the task, that either they or the task's value to the organization should be overlooked. The compounding costs of these opportunities and challenges of invisible work have been reflected in McKinsey & Company 2023 Women in the Workplace Report,[25] when underrepresented individuals were more broadly represented at the bottom of the organization chart in supportive, administrative, and service roles.

Mirrors

Reflecting on how our interactions with others have been informed by our own experiences, whether limited or limitless, shaping our perspectives, biases, and stereotypes. Every day people walk into a room, and they are the only one, while others have never experienced such a moment. So tolerance waivers for some and resilience builds for others. Therefore, we must **be critically conscious**. Do not accept and default to what has always been. Reality check — It is broken! Recognizing that our reality is not another's reality, we must see beyond our own personal experience by being reflective, open, and intentional. Being critically aware of all the information we receive, who we receive it from, and where we receive it.

Recognizing if there is a pattern. Challenging ourselves to listen to other unheard voices and stories, which will help foster a deeper understanding of the world about you. Think about two people that are different from you in some way, whether in lived experiences or demographics, and consider their daily interactions. How could they be similar and how could they be dissimilar?

Today, performatively signaling change will no longer work, so **infrastructure must be built, and resources allocated**. Be the change that you want to see. Always question the status quo. Asking why and why not. If the structure has been broken for a decade, even decades, should we really expect the new savior to have it fixed within six months? Examine the current infrastructure and ask if it advantages some people, while disadvantages others. Recognizing that people and their time are our greatest resource, how could one improve the infrastructure to make it more effective for the greater good? Gaining buy-in and instilling trust

takes relentless time, grace, commitment, and resources.

Our (In)visible Work

Fight for the things that you care about, but do it in a way that will lead others to join you.
Ruth Bader Ginsburg, Former Supreme Court Justice

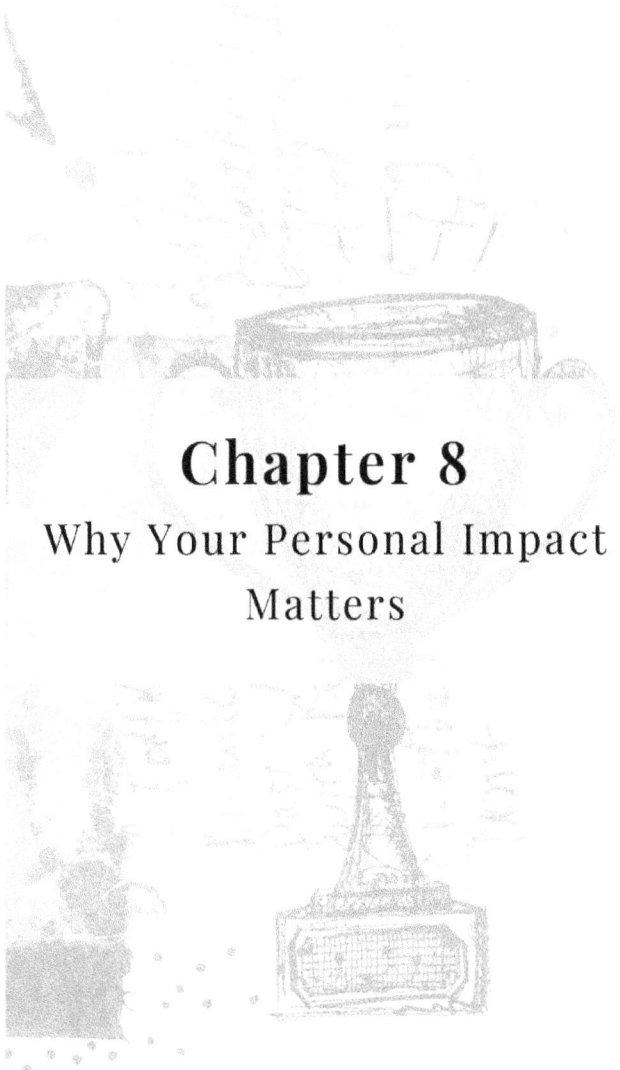

Chapter 8
Why Your Personal Impact Matters

8: Why Your Personal Impact Matters

When was the last time you:

- **Made yourself a priority?**

- **Advocated for yourself?**

- **Held a boundary to protect your well-being?**

- **Celebrated your successes?**

In a world hungry for authenticity, our personal impact is the compass guiding a legacy that transcends time. Your impact is not confined to calendars and spreadsheets; it is an imprint of your dedication, your willingness to support others, and your capacity to inspire change. It is the catalyst for fostering camaraderie, trust, and infusing vitality back into the work. Every time we're knocked down by work or life — whether due to mistakes, lessons, sickness, or the death of a loved one — we quickly learn that we can drop a lot of things, if and when needed. It is suddenly possible to:

- say no to requests

- ask for help

- cancel redundant meetings

- eliminate unwanted obligations

- take care of ourselves

- advocate for ourselves

- eventually re-evaluate what we want in life and how we want to be treated.

Our (In)visible Work

Self-advocacy is defined as the "ability to communicate one's needs and wants and to make decisions about the supports necessary to achieve them."[1] If we go back to the introduction and the concept of the socially constructed world, the expectations, norms, and rules by which we live are ever changing. They are also of our own making, so we may have some control over the way we interact with the world and the rules by which we choose to govern ourselves. The first step in this, however, is making sure we know and give words to the invisible work that is impeding our personal growth. Can we self-advocate before becoming resentful? Can we love ourselves enough to reassess the situation, ignore social norms, and speak up to champion ourselves? Jacqueline reflects on the importance of reminding herself to have control over how we interact with the world around us and react to it.

A teacher introduced me to Roosevelt's quote 'No one can make you feel inferior without your consent' during a rough patch in my youth. In hindsight, I can acknowledge it was a mixture of bullying and imposter syndrome that impacted me, and this quote shared by a trusted mentor made all the difference in the world. It gave me the courage to take my goals, aspirations, and happiness into my own hands. As an adult, I have revisited this quote time and time again to remind myself that *I* have to be the one who believes in me.

Jacqueline. 40. Academic. #AlwaysLearning

This theme of having to be one's own champion emerged from

our interviews and discussions. Regardless of one's career stage, both Caroline and Khalil had realizations of the need to advocate for themselves.

> If I don't champion for myself, then who? And when? Even after my history-making two million in sales, I am constantly told I have to wait my turn. Yet, look at my record.
>
> **Caroline. 20s. Sales Associate. #DogMom**

Six months on the job, Caroline brought in over $2 million worth of sales. That was more than most of her peers with even more years of experience. However, without the lack of advocacy from her supervisors, she still felt her growth was being limited. Similarly, Khalil recognized throughout his 15 years of experience that no one is a better advocate for him than himself.

> Advocating for myself and others is a two-edged sword, you know. Personally, over the years I continued to move that ball forward, so yes, I dressed differently. I did my hair differently, but honestly when I'm talking to people now, I've told them I'm tired of toning down. I have done all the hoops and played all the games. I'm tired of waiting for someone else to advocate for me. I am comfortable with who I am. It is a reminder for me, and it paves a new path for the next.
>
> **Khalil. 40s. Operations Executive. #GirlDad**

Our (In)visible Work

Structural factors like the criminal justice, healthcare, and educational systems influence persistent inequities,[2, 3, 4] and we must tirelessly work to dismantle, reimagine, and restructure these systems. We must also recognize, own, and adjust what we *can* control and change. For example, in education, if we want our service contributions to be more visible, then we need to bring more visibility to the invisible service work. Both Joy and Georgia entered established systems and found ways to manage what they could.

> At our institution, service is 5% of my workload — which equates to two hours a week. Yet, service includes advising students, leading student trips, stewarding program partnerships, assisting fellowships, reviewing manuscripts, serving on program, college, and university committees, so I started to track my hours, so I could better advocate with data.
>
> **Joy. 40s. Professor. #LatinaBoyMom**

Similar to Joy, Georgia recognized she was doing excessive service work and had to find a way to bring attention to her colleagues and administration.

> As an art teacher, I enrich all 500+ students at our school. So, when we have parent conference days, I don't just have 25 students to focus on. I have twenty times that amount. Now, I can't control how the system

was initially set up; however, I have helped bring a new perspective to change the system.

Georgia. 50s. Artist. #UberMom

When Self-Advocacy and Individual Advocacy Evolves into System Advocacy

Generally, "advocacy" connotes championing a cause or seeking outcomes and resources. Conversely, "assertion" connotes championing and demanding resources, recognition, or rewards for yourself. In every country, men have traditionally held roles enhanced by their assertiveness (e.g., competitive breadwinner, authoritative parent, powerful supervisor), while women have been expected to act as advocates (e.g., encouraging partner, prodding parent, supportive colleague).[5, 6] Jocelyn's insights from her experiences climbing the professional ladder of being an American football referee made her realize she had to advocate for herself.

I am more mindful of having to credit myself. I learned quickly when I wasn't getting selected or promoted. I always got swept up in the team's job well done, that I personally got lost, so now I reference the team accomplishments and my personal contributions.

Jocelyn. 30s. American Football Referee. #BlackWomenInSport

Once again, these stereotyped, gender-linked norms and expectations — such as modesty and selflessness — remain surprisingly current and, despite some significant changes in the workplace, appear to be influenced by patriarchal societies and family socialization.[5, 6, 7] Each of these traditional definitions has limitations: advocacy does not imply advocacy for oneself, and assertion does imply the inclusion of others. Those who have not asserted themselves are described as lacking confidence in their beliefs, feelings, and opinions. Those who do not ask for resources could be seen as lacking confidence; however, those who champion someone else's cause can have great conviction in their beliefs.

Given the limitations of "advocacy" and "assertion," newer terminology has been introduced. Society is moving from self-advocacy and individual advocacy to more inclusive terms like systems advocacy.[8] To distinguish among the advocacies:

- self-advocacy depicts the power and influence leveraged for one's self;

- individual advocacy characterizes the power and influence used for others;

- systems advocacy is focused on changing laws, policies, or rules.

Historically, one's identity has been accompanied by a level of comfort and confidence. For example, women have typically been more comfortable and effective using individual advocacy because it involves making requests for other individuals and not for themselves. Conversely, the self-promotion influence in self-advocacy has, traditionally, been performed by men.[9, 10] Here we go again with these prescribed gender roles trapping our thinking, limiting societal expectations, and possibly diminishing our own advocacy.

It would be short-sighted of us to identify the conditions for which one, generally someone from an underrepresented group, acts as a self-advocate without fear of reprisal. After all, most of the research and all these personal stories suggest it is not wise simply to encourage the marginalized to ignore the repercussions of their out-of-role behaviors. Maybe there's an alternative to imagine moving from individualized advocacy to systems advocacy. That is, a Black woman's self-advocacy might be seen as more socially acceptable if the request for herself were tempered by a simultaneous request for others — for example, as a supervisor requesting equitable salaries for all in her department, including herself. Or as a breast cancer survivor advocating for greater funding and research to benefit every cancer patient. Yes, systems advocacy seems redundant of the lay meaning of advocacy; however, it signals a shared effort. It signals inclusion. It signals belongingness.

The Role of Power and Influence in Advocacy

Power and influence are particularly relevant when discussing advocacy,[5, 8] and yet these two words are difficult to distinguish from one another.[9, 11, 12] Although advocates are influential, they generally may not hold much power; however, advocacy generally occurs within a power structure. Think of the manager of a small department. While they may not have the most power within the organization as a whole, they can act as an advocate for the department and influence other powerful individuals to obtain resources. Researchers argue power signals control and coercion over people, resources, or outcomes, while influence connotes a softer persuasion without the use of coercion.[11, 12] Interestingly, researchers continue to investigate if one's power or ability to influence emerges from their organizational position, their social capital, their interpersonal relationships, their personality characteristics, their leadership behaviors, or a combination of these. Such combinations come close to describing a partnership. Now, imagine if we reframed advocacy as a partnership? Palatable, possibly. Empowering, definitely.

Picture an executive who is well-liked and respected by internal and external stakeholders, a highly conscious individual with a collaborative approach. Is that combination more likely to influence others compared to an executive with a narcissistic personality and an autocratic approach? Now, there is no explicit answer because we only described the person, so we cannot lose sight of the organizational life cycle, the societal, economical, and political climates, but we hope you get the point.

Until the 21st century, the recipient of the advocacy attempt was overlooked by researchers. The focus of power and influence research switched from *what* to *whom*. Answering questions like:

- Who will benefit from the request?
- For whom do individuals request resources?
- For whom do individuals request rewards?

Our (In)visible Work

When these questions are answered, it helps identify the conditions in which people are more comfortable and effective advocates. Researchers discovered leaders with higher needs and commitment for socialized power versus personalized power were stronger assets to one another and to the organization. Another reason to redistribute the power and reframe advocacy as a partnership.

Mirrors

Recognize that there is not enough room in that beautiful mind of yours to remember wins from a year ago, so **document your accomplishments and value**. No matter how big or small a win is a win. Print out critical emails applauding your work, create a win folder, record key projects you impacted, and obstacles you encountered and resolved. **Know your values, and never compromise them.** Your personal brand and reputation are worth more in the long term than any potential gain to be had in the short term, so be committed to never compromising your most important values. Develop a personal constitution. What are the guiding principles that will help you achieve what you want to achieve and be the person you want to be? Never sacrifice your integrity for personal gains or the gains of others. **Sing your praise. Sing their praise. Sing our praise.** Speak up, even if your voice shakes. Sometimes you'll hear no, but you won't know unless you ask — whether it's for that promotion, a higher salary, time for yourself, a more efficient process, or a new hire to support the team.

140

Our (In)visible Work

The sage does not hoard. Having bestowed all he has on others, he has yet more; having given all he has to others, he is richer still.
Lao Tzu, Philosopher

Chapter 9
Why Your Allyship Can Create the New Invisible Economy

9: Why Your Allyship Can Create the New Invisible Economy

How do you react when someone tells you that you've hurt them?

How do you react when someone tells you the system is broken?

How are you leveraging your advantages to help others?

Since the moment George Floyd was murdered in 2020, there has been a renewed movement for allyship. Some started with sharing social messages, attending parades and rallies, and donating to causes. And yes, these were all great starting points; however, the reality is that allyship takes long-term commitment and, at times, uncomfortable but necessary — say it with us — invisible work.

Let's define ally and allyship. An ally is an individual "who strives to end oppression through supporting and advocating on behalf of the oppressed."[1] Typically, allies are those with advantages who leverage their status to enact positive change. For example, an able-bodied individual may be an ally for a person with a differing ability, a heterosexual person may be an ally for someone in the lesbian, gay, bisexual, transgender, and queer (LGBTQ+) community, a man may be an ally for a woman, or a native speaking person may be an ally for a multilingual person. Jocelyn recalls the allyship of her professor.

My first graduate school internship almost made me quit school and that career pursuit. I constantly experienced microaggressions and was even told I should return to my "shithole" country. I finally went to my professor. She listened to me. She heard me. She valued me, and she immediately stepped up to act.

Jocelyn. 30s. American Football Referee. #BlackWomenInSport

Like Jocelyn, Caroline experienced an ally who actively listened to her experiences and needs without taking over or speaking for her.

After a year on this committee, finally I had someone who actually listened and centered my voice and didn't just try to speak for me.

Caroline. 20s. Sales Associate. #DogMom

For an ally to move into allyship, individuals must actively, consistently, and arduously practice learning, unlearning, and relearning where the systemic power is oppressing individuals and stand in solidarity with the oppressed group to remove the system that challenges their basic rights.[2, 3] Researchers remind us that we each have an area in which we can practice allyship because everyone holds some form of systemic power in some areas and lacks it in others.[4, 5] And nope, there aren't breaks in allyship. Remember people from oppressed groups don't have a choice whether or not to deal with the daily oppressions, so neither should you as an ally.

Being active and authentic is vital to allyship. When someone exemplifies inauthentic displays of support, it is known as performative allyship. Performative allyship, while appearing supportive on the surface, often lacks genuine commitment or substantial action toward advocating for marginalized communities.[6, 7] One common instance of performative allyship is social media posts and hashtags to show solidarity with a cause without engaging in tangible actions or education about the issues at hand. Similarly, organizations may engage in performative allyship gestures when they temporarily change brands or slogans without implementing concrete internal changes to address systemic inequalities. For example, once a year adding rainbow filters to support LGBTQ+ movements, yet not addressing your exclusionary policies is a surface level act. These "window dressing" instances highlight how performative allyship often prioritizes optics over genuine support and fails to contribute meaningfully to dismantling systemic injustices.

Even prior to having a formal definition, the idea of allies and allyship has been discussed by scholars and practiced by humans for decades, even centuries ago during the Underground Railroad in the 1800s and across many contexts. Allyship is a particularly useful cross-cultural tool. Across the diverse world, there are differing types and amounts of discrimination, prejudice, and laws, yet the effect is generally influenced by the region of the world.[6, 7, 8, 9] Allyship can then be a universal tool to help in all contexts, regardless of the type of discrimination or legal protections available. As such, allyship education and programming would be a useful tool for all initiatives.

According to Lean In's research,[10] more than 80% of white employees see themselves as allies in the workplace, yet only 45% of

Our (In)visible Work

Black women and 55% of Latina women agree that they have workplace allies. Speaking specifically about racial discrimination at work, only four in ten White employees report speaking up. So why is there a disconnect in perceptions of self- reporting as an ally and recognized allyship? Remember that being an ally isn't a status that's self-identified or concretely attained. Allyship is a process that requires constant commitment and work.

Historically, researchers have examined why an individual becomes an ally[11] and how allies take action,[12] yet rarely do scholars examine the assumption that an ally engages in advocacy to transform existing social relations for the disadvantage. We do know that disadvantaged group members unwaveringly participate in action to improve the status of their own disadvantaged group.[13] Yet far less attention has been paid to examining the participation of advantaged group members in these actions.[14, 15] Both Danielle and Khalil recall examples where women were spoken over in meetings and an ally stepped into action.

This just happened the other day: my co-worker interrupted me and explained the topic from his perspective as though his thoughts were more important than mine. And then, an ally at the table, who was another man, stepped in and said, "Let Danielle finish talking."

Danielle. 50s. Director. #ClimbingEnthusiast

I am surrounded by strong confident women — my mother, godmother, wife, sisters, colleagues, and daughters. And I realized or shall I say someone did remind me once that I was talking over them. Ever since, I consciously restrain myself. I also have no problem correcting others.

Khalil. 40s. Operations Executive. #GirlDad

Our (in)visible economy will not disappear; however, it must evolve with nurturing from your allyship. Our society needs people who are doing the little things that make our lives more organized, manageable, and frankly enjoyable. A new (in)visible economy would prioritize and acknowledge the multifaceted contributions and perspectives of all groups.[16] Such an approach will foster innovation and creativity by drawing upon a wider range of experiences and insights.[17] Moreover, an (in)visible economy rooted in allyship will engender trust, collaboration, and social cohesion, which will foster a more sustainable environment.[18] The new (in)visible economy isn't solely about transactions and profit margins; it's a collective commitment to building sustainable, resilient communities where every individual's contribution is valued and celebrated — a testament to the power of allyship in shaping a thriving, inclusive economic future.

Mirrors

Your impact is greater than your intentions, so get ready to make mistakes. **You will make mistakes.** Ruminating on mistakes is a disservice to yourself. Apologize, learn from it, and move on.

Acknowledging mistakes shows that you are accountable and willing to learn. Do not ask for emotional energy for your mistake, the historically marginalized group is not obligated to like you, feel sorry for you, forgive you, or thank you. **Acknowledge your preconceived thinking, your limited awareness, and your bias.** Although mentioned before in chapter 7, we feel it's important to include a second time because everyone makes assumptions and is unconsciously biased. To interpret the world around us, our bounded rationality requires that we make shortcuts to process and categorize information quickly. Thus, we need to ensure, however, that the biases resulting from these shortcuts are not absolutes and that we acknowledge the impact they have on our day-to-day interactions with people. Then **educate yourself**. If your first response is to go to a marginalized individual and ask them, "What should I do? What should I read? Where should I go?" then you're looking in the wrong place. Questions like this put the burden and responsibility on the person who is *already* burdened. Instead, **take initiative** by doing your own research — read a book, listen to a podcast, watch a TedxTalk, take a LinkedIn Learning course. Then act and share what you've learned with others and continue building upon that. Remember there are no checkbox lists or one size fits all. Rather, it's an ongoing action, every day, everywhere.

Our (In)visible Work

Part 4: HOW to Bring Value and Voice to the Unseen

Do the best you can until you know better. Then when you know better, do better.
Maya Angelou, Author

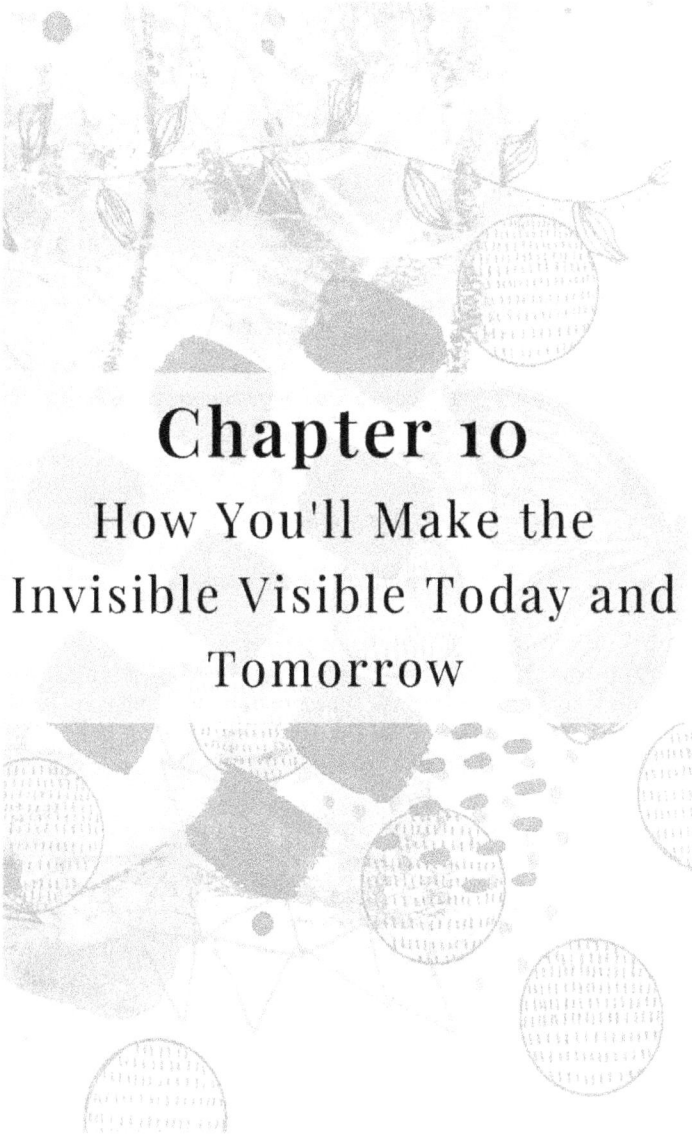

Chapter 10
How You'll Make the Invisible Visible Today and Tomorrow

Our (In)visible Work
10: How You'll Make the Invisible

Visible Today and Tomorrow How often do you:

- **Listen to your internal mental dialogue?**

- **Rethink what you've always thought to be true?**

- **Intentionally question the systems by which society operates?**

- **Recognize your perception is not another's reality?**

Forty years post-inception of the term "invisible work," we have hit a tipping point — better yet, a boiling point — making inaction or ignorance no longer options. You can no longer unsee the visible. Since the pandemic put intense pressure to recognize burnout, quiet quitting, and boundaries, it is mission critical that we meet this moment, acknowledge the invisible work, and value those efforts. Ultimately, the presence of (in)visible work is inevitable. Acknowledging and valuing (in)visible labor is not just an act of recognition; it's a testament to our interdependence as a society. It's a reminder that we all play a role, seen or unseen, in maintaining the delicate balance of our world. In such a world, perhaps we would cherish and appreciate the hidden efforts that make our lives possible with a newfound awareness and gratitude. As we mentioned in the book introduction there will always be loose threads in the fabric of our lives. They are reminders of our humanity — an invitation to explore, reflect, and make choices. Remember whether we choose to ignore, mend, or free ourselves, the act of acknowledging the loose thread is a step toward better understanding ourselves and others.

Our (In)visible Work

Like the dualities of work and life, where one can feel both visible and invisible at once, we must render all forms of work. For example, when the token Black woman, responsible for retail sales in the mid-western region of the U.S., hosts a panel on anti-racism in the wake of workplace racial upheaval, we can no longer just applaud her for her passion work, but we must also reward her for her leadership efforts, strategic planning abilities, additional time, and DEI acumen. Instead, we must know the markers of valued work: recognition and reward. And if this token individual's efforts go unnoticed or unrewarded, again we effectively render the invisible work with no to low status and value. Now of course, Black women have historically done this invisible work (see chapter 7), however, it continues to result in the minority/cultural tax. Coined by educational researcher Amado Padilla[1] in 1994, the term "cultural taxation" is a tax of extra responsibilities historically placed on ethnic minorities who carry out duties because of their ethno-racial backgrounds.

Throughout the book, we have shared stories and research of how the tax of invisible work has been amplified by the following factors: constraints on time, professional norms, inequitable resources, emotional labor, lack of allyship, and expectations of a gratitude tax or a feeling of obligation to be grateful for any opportunities gotten. To offset the invisible economy, we must create tools and metrics to measure what once was invisible work, ensuring avenues to value and promote. We must revise or replace procedures or policies that contribute to structural inequity. Recognizing such efforts will enlarge the pool of people willing to contribute their time, effort, and talent, setting the stage for change. We must actively recruit or redistribute, instead of always expecting and seeing the same people serving invisible work. These measures will help build capacity and work towards building a better future for the invisible work.

Through this book's journey, our hope is that you have better language to identify invisible work, and everyone has a better understanding of the challenges it creates for not only you, but also your colleagues, partners, friends, neighbors, and children. We hope you connected with a few of these stories and now have strategies to help move your invisible work and that of others from invisible to visible. In the ongoing, often fraught march to recognize invisible work, the pandemic made the weight of added duties — like caring for a sick family member, feeding one's family, finding work during widespread layoffs, and taking on homeschooling — even heavier and more glaring to those tasked with them. As we rebuild our new normal in this world, this is your opportunity to choose how you as an individual move forward and co-exist. Andre encourages us to optimistically choose to be a voice and reflection for change.

Even today, without my white coat, some view me as suspicious. Clinching their purse in the elevator. Not much has changed in 20 years when I was falsely treated like a criminal by police officers as a Black 16-year-old boy and reduced to nothing. We're past the time of rewriting the stereotypical script. Be a picture of change. Be a reflection for change. Be a voice for change.

Andre. 30s. Doctor. #FunUncle

As we conclude, we want to acknowledge the monumental task of changing how our society views and values invisible work. Uncovering all the facets of invisible work amid our uniqueness will take time. Stay strong. Stay committed. Stay resilient. We are on the verge of change. Think of work as an iceberg. If we consider the part above the water as work that's currently valued and paid, and what is below the water as all the aspects that are invisible, we essentially are asking to flip the iceberg. If you have ever seen an iceberg flip, you know it is usually when a piece has broken off from the main iceberg. A lot of waves result from this process called calving, and it's actually quite a beautiful sight to behold. This change is dramatic and dynamic. In looking to uncover the invisible work, we need to break off from the mainstream view of what work is and how we value it. We will make waves with far-reaching impacts.

Continue the Journey: Join Our (In)visible Work Community

To maintain the momentum, join our online forum at wellsquest.com/ourinvisiblework. There, you will be part of a community

Our (In)visible Work

bringing visibility to the invisible, where you can share your invisible work stories and strategies, adopt resources and tools for your continued journey (or maybe help jump start the journey for your curious or clueless colleague, friend, or partner). The journey continues with a podcast, Our (In)visible Work, where we will learn together, unpacking these themes and discovering new themes. When writing this book, we wanted to acknowledge that everyone has some invisible work, and therefore, this is an issue that's important for all people to embrace and explore. Our future work will tell the specific stories of individuals and their roles in the workplace and society. In the meantime, we hope that you will consider this book as a starting point on a journey to better appreciate ourselves and those around us, together making the world better through the invisible work we do.

Mirrors

Give agency. Before assuming someone's willingness or capacity for tasks or engagements, ask them directly and respectfully. This cultivates a habit of giving agency to others and respecting their autonomy. Ask, invite, request, and do so with an open mind. Some individuals may be energized by work; some people may be exhausted by the work. Assume neither a desire nor an obligation for anyone. **Recognize and reward.** Gain a better understanding of the work you and others do. Through this, you can continuously give encouragement and foster a deeper sense of purpose. Ask people how they like to be recognized and

158

rewarded. Share how you like to be recognized and rewarded. Build this into the evaluation and compensation structure. Move from "thank you for volunteering" to "here is the value you and your work add." **Forge ahead fearlessly.** Remember fear is false evidence appearing real and it surfaces when challenged with the desire for disruption, so rock the boat. Shake up the status quo.

Work is love made visible.
Kahlil Gibran, Poet

Our (In)visible Work
About the Authors

Janelle

Growing up in Satellite Beach, Florida, I was blissfully ignorant to the work my single mother did while I was sleeping, practicing multiple sports, and going to school — and to think that was only the house labor my mother performed. I can only imagine the invisible work she did in the workforce as a partially deaf Latina woman. Shoot, 40 years later, *I'm* still experiencing a misogynist workplace. But, wow, did my mother prevail far greater than her immigrant Cuban and Dominican parents could have ever dreamed.

Today, as a mother myself, raising three active boys with my life partner, educating the next generation as a professor, growing a business with WellsQuest, and trying to be a thoughtful sister and friend, I am not the only one who wears many hats; however, how can we best communicate to ensure we see one another, and, better yet, we see and value the work we are each doing?

Our (In)visible Work is a long overdue creation, inspired by my students, my mother, my sister, my colleagues, and my husband. During office hours, as I shed tears with students enduring racist, sexist, homophobic harassment during their graduate school internships, I listened to their stories, valuing them. And I strived to ensure their workplace improved in valuing them, too. Together, it is everyone's responsibility to make the world more inclusive. If you hear about a problem, it's your duty to do something about it.

As a professor, I've strategized with my colleagues on how to navigate the labyrinth of higher education politics that continues to reward the most self-interested individuals yet proclaims to be serving students first. And for the last decade, I have worked to ensure my department chair, deans, and provosts see the service to my students deserves more than 5% of my time.

As a former collegiate athlete and coach turned sport educator and consultant, I've confronted the sexist, male-prevalent industry of sports and entertainment with the best of friends, particularly my sister, Eryn, who has 20+ years pushing creative boundaries working for sport marketing agencies and properties. Although the industry can be so progressive on the field, pitch, ice, or court, behind the curtain of business, it is one of the most archaic patriarchal systems in existence. And I relentlessly work to make it better for the next generation, particularly the next generation of female sports and entertainment industry leaders. I've shared the good, the bad, and the uglier with them

161

so they're better prepared to navigate all the obstacles (yes, the invisible work), with the blissful hope they can unapologetically pave their own paths as strong, direct, assertive women who deserve to be in *that* room and at *that* table. And if there isn't a seat at that table, you bring a seat for yourself and the person next to you.

As a mother, I've laughed with my mommy groups discussing our self-enabling childcare and household habits and demands that may be causing us more work. Reminding myself and others that we can do it our way and allow others to do it their way. Neither one is wrong, but all are correct. Goodness, folks, let's be content that the work is completed.

As a partner, my husband constantly navigates dual career paths with me, while we raise three African American Latino boys in systems — whether corporate, political, or educational — not designed by us or for us. We're also in a sandwich era, more like a panini, advocating for our aging parents. Through it all we challenge and support one another to remain steadfast and hopeful, even at the most frustrating times, unequivocally believing that together, we will go farther.

Today, as a friend, sister, auntie, mother, daughter, wife, author, scholar, consultant, and, most notably, educator at heart, it is my hope and responsibility to share and extend knowledge through *Our (In)visible Work*. As the activist and poet Maya Angelou eloquently stated, "When you know better, do better." May we all do better making invisible work visible.

Doreen

There are many parts of my story that have brought me to be involved in this project. I will start first with my family. I was raised by parents in Nova Scotia, Canada, and they very much aligned the roles they played in their marriage with the idea that the mother did the domestic work like cooking, cleaning, handling the children's schedules — and the father worked as the main breadwinner with household responsibilities like the yardwork, mechanical work, and handling the finances. My sister and I, however, were never expected to adhere to the same roles. In fact, quite the opposite: My mother saw and understood that the value of her societal contribution didn't equal that of my father, and that was her motivation to see her children never be bound to antiquated norms.

My realization of this inequity, however, was something I only began to understand when my mother started to work on a local ferry. She always worked outside of the home when we were growing up, but when she started to work two weeks at sea and then two weeks at home, it was a reality check. We saw the double duty she was maintaining. The reason she was always the last to bed now makes sense to us.

Once I started working and living on my own, the duality of paid work and unpaid work became even more apparent. While working in the hospitality industry, I remember one executive telling me that to be successful in the industry, I needed to know there would be sacrifices. She brought to my attention that all the people I aspired to be like were unwillingly single or divorced. And for those who had families, they were on the verge of burning out. She explained that because of the effort required to have a successful career and a family, expecting both was unrealistic.

Since family, community, and work were all important to me, I decided to change my circumstances and found a profession that allowed for balance and enough room for happiness. I built a life with a loving spouse. In developing our life, however, my partner and I have struggled. We have had to learn how to be very open with our communication about the balance we seek. I feel fortunate to have a spouse who is willing to challenge the status quo as much as I am. Our push to create our own type of relationship balance allowed me to go back to school to build the life I wanted.

While pursuing my doctorate in business administration, I found myself among a group of critical management scholars who questioned the same things I did about the unrealistic expectations and inequities in our society — most poignant of which was the realization that the divide over what's monetarily valued in society and not monetarily valued was socially constructed, not absolute. It led me to further question what could be done to better understand the inequities caused by how we value one type of work over another.

I wondered if in the pursuit of finding a place in the paid workplace, women had further marginalized and devalued the domestic roles people were playing in society. I wanted to explore turning points in society where choices were made to place value on certain activities and how different choices have potentially brought about a recognition of unpaid work conducted in our society. One of my advisers at the time, a world-renowned scholar in the social sciences, suggested that such a study would perhaps be better off as a work of fiction, as this concept would be too difficult to research. It was discouraging. And although I found other topics to research as a scholar, this remained a question for me.

A few years after graduating with my doctorate, when I started working and researching with Dr. Wells, she told me of her idea for a book on (in)visible work. She wanted to explore the missing value of work that was unseen. This was a means to study the questions I had. Excitedly, we started to explore, and we realized this was so much bigger than a gender issue. Frankly speaking, as a white cisgendered individual, I enjoy certain privileges that make much of the invisible work we've uncovered unknown to me, which made my desire to learn even more palpable. Invisible work comes in many forms in the workplace, in our communities, and within people's families. People are expected to complete tasks and play roles for which they are not recognized or remunerated all the time. It is our hope, through this project, to help all of us see and appreciate the invisible work of others.

About the Illustrator: Galina Fouks-Abele

Galina grew up in Chicago and spent any free time at her family cabin in the northern woods of Wisconsin, where she feels spiritually rooted and grounded as an adult. She received a BA in fine arts and a volleyball scholarship at the University of South Florida where she was on the Dean's List and was honored with MVP, NCAA, and school records. She received a BA from Georgia State University in art education and a master's in education school leadership from Touro College in New York City. Galina has been teaching since 1995 and for the past 29 years floated between administration and her love of teaching art. Her work as an educator is not bounded by the classroom walls. And she has experienced the invisible work of serving students with enduring compassion, theatrical lessons, and relentless inspiration.

Outside the classroom, Galina is an author, illustrator, camp curator, and professional artist, creating art for private and public commissions worldwide. She has shared her talents with the world by publishing and illustrating four books ranging in topics about grief, self-confidence, and child anxiety. She and her husband stay busy connecting their community and empowering the next generation, particularly their daughter. Galina's most treasured gift is her ability to see the beauty in everything and bring it to life for people to see.

When asked, "What invisible work is included in your artistry?," she noted it isn't so much the work of the art but having the vision first. She states, "I can see the image before I paint or draw it. Often, when I am creating the piece intuitively, I can feel it forming with my paint and I know it is happening as it should. I cannot start it unless I have the vision. That is some of the invisible work I must do."

You can reach her on Instagram @galinaabeleart @tampaartteachermrsabele or via email at galinajf1@aol.com.

References

Preface

1. Mahajan, D., White, O., Madgavkar, A., & Krishnan, M. (2020, September 16). *Don't let the pandemic set back gender equality.* Harvard Business Review. https://hbr.org/2020/09/dont- let-the-pandemic-set-back-gender-equality

2. Dugarova, E. (2020, June). *Unpaid care work in times of the COVID-19 crisis: Gendered impacts, emerging evidence and promising policy responses.* United Nations. https://www.un.org/development/desa/family/wp-content/uploads/sites/23/2020/09/Duragova.Paper_.pdf

3. OECD. (2021, December 13). *Caregiving in crisis: Gender inequality in paid and unpaid work during COVID-19.* OECD.org. https://www.oecd.org/coronavirus/policy- responses/caregiving-in-crisis-gender-inequality-in-paid-and-unpaid-work-during-covid-19-3555d164/

4. Ferrant, G., Pesando, L. M., & Nowacka, K. (2014, December). *Unpaid care work: The missing link in the analysis of gender gaps in labour outcomes.* OECD Development Centre. https://www.oecd.org/dev/development-gender/Unpaid_care_work.pdf

5. Emens, E. (2018, December 5). *The invisible labor of life admin.* Psychology Today. https://www.psychologytoday.com/us/blog/life-admin/201812/the-invisible-labor-life-admin

6. Wells, J. E., & MacAulay, D. (2024, June 10). *What 'invisible work' looks like in the 21st century.* Psychology Today. https://www.psychologytoday.com/us/blog/our-invisible-work/202406/what-invisible-work-looks-like-in-the-21st-century

7. Rodsky, E. (2021). *Fair play: A game-changing solution for when you have too much to do (and more life to live).* Penguin Publishing Group.

8. Hochschild, A. R. (1983). *The managed heart: Commercialization of human feeling.* University of California Press.

9. McGee, E. O., & Martin, D. B. (2011). "You would not believe what I have to go through to prove my intellectual value!" Stereotype management among academically successful Black mathematics and engineering students. *American Educational Research Journal, 48*(6), 1347-1389.

10. Motro, D., Evans, J. B., Ellis, A. P. J., & Benson, L., III (2021). Race and reactions to women's expressions of anger at work: Examining the effects of the "Angry Black Woman" stereotype. *Journal of Applied Psychology, 107*, 142-152.

11. Canizales, S. L., & Hondagneu-Sotelo, P. (2022). Working-class Latina/o youth navigating stratification and inequality: A review of literature. *Sociology Compass*, 1-15.

12. Hsieh, Y., Sonmez, S., Apostolopoulos, Y., & Lemke, M. (2017). Perceived workplace mistreatment: Case of Latina hotel housekeepers. *Works, 56*(1), 55-65.
13. Ye Hee Lee, M. (2024, February 21). *South Korea, a nation of rigid gender norms, meets its changemakers.* The Washington Post. https://www.washingtonpost.com/world/2024/02/21/south-korea-women-gender-equality- gap/
14. Gupta, A., Szymanski, D. M., & Leong, F. T. L. (2011). The "model minority myth": Internalized racialism of positive stereotypes as correlates of psychological distress, and attitudes toward help-seeking. *Asian American Journal of Psychology, 2*, 101–14.
15. Rosie Report. (2022, June). *The 3rd annual Rosie report.* We are Rosie. https://wearerosie.com/therosie-report/
16. Mazzuca, C., Majid, A., Lugli, L., Nicoletti, R., & Borghi, A. M. (2020). Gender is a multifaceted concept: Evidence that specific life experiences differentially shape the concept of gender. *Language and Cognition, 12*(4), 649–678.
17. Perez, C. C. (2019). *Invisible Women: Data bias in a world designed for men.* Abrams Press.

Introduction

1. Bourdieu, P. (1977). *Outline of a theory of Practice.* Cambridge University Press.
2. Frone, M.R., Russell, M., & Cooper, M. L. (1992). Antecedents and outcomes of work- family conflict: Testing a model of the work-family interface. *Journal of Applied Psychology, 77*, 65-78.
3. Greenhaus, J. H., Parasuraman, S., Granrose, C. I. K., Rabinowitz, S., Beutell, N. J. (1989). Sources of work-family conflict among two-career couples. *Journal of Vocational Behavior, 34*, 133-53.
4. Han, G. H., Lee, J. H., & Chin, M. J. (2009). Changes in Korean families and child development. *Journal of Korean Association of Childs Study, 30*(6), 1-14.
5. Harrington, F., Van Deusen, & Fraone, J. S. (2013). *The new dad: A work (and life) in progress.* Boston College Center for Work & Family. https://www.bc.edu/content/dam/files/centers/cwf/research/fatherhood/BCCWF%20The%20 New%20Dad%20(2013).pdf
6. Suttie, J. (2019, November 5). *How an unfair division of labor hurts your relationship.* Greater Good. https://greatergood.berkeley.edu/article/item/how_an_unfair_division_of_labor_hurts_your_relationship
7. Daniels, A. K. (1987). Invisible work. *Social Problems, 34*(5), 403-415.
8. Emens, E. (2018, December 5). *The invisible labor of life admin.* Psychology Today. https://www.psychologytoday.com/us/blog/life-admin/201812/the-invisible-labor-life-admin

9. Wells, J. E., & MacAulay, D. (2024, June 10). *What 'invisible work' looks like in the 21st century*. Psychology Today. https://www.psychologytoday.com/us/blog/our-invisible-work/202406/what-invisible-work-looks-like-in-the-21st-century

10. Klotz, A. C., & Bolino, M. C. (2016). Saying goodbye: The nature, causes, and consequences of employee resignation styles. *Journal of Applied Psychology, 101*(10), 1386.

11. Seedat, S., & Rondon, M. (2021). Women's wellbeing and the burden of unpaid work. *BMJ*, 374.

12. Grossman, J. (n.d.). *Fair labor standards act of 1938: Maximum struggle for a minimum wage*. U.S. Department of Labor. https://www.dol.gov/general/aboutdol/history/flsa1938

13. U.S. Department of Labor. (2018, January). *Fact Sheet #71: Internships programs under the fair labor standards act*. U.S. Department of Labor. https://www.dol.gov/agencies/whd/fact-sheets/71-flsa-internships

Chapter 1

1. Rogers, C. (1961). On becoming a person: A therapist's view of psychotherapy. Houghton Mifflin.

2. Avolio, B. J., & Gardner, W. L. (2005). Authentic leadership development: getting to the root of positive forms of leadership. *The Leadership Quarterly*, 16(3), 315-338.

3. Grant, A. (2023, September 17). *Authenticity is not about expressing every opinion you hold. It's about ensuring that what you voice reflects what you value*. Twitter. https://twitter.com/AdamMGrant/status/1703427240178958586

4. MacAulay, K. D. (2013). *The modernized public servant: a poststructuralist perspective on the 'modernization' of the Canadian public service*. Saint Mary's University.

5. Hopkins, E. (1982). Working hours and conditions during the industrial revolution: A re- appraisal. *The Economic History Review, 35*(1), 52-66.

6. Kühn, S., Horne, R., Yoon, S., & Rafferty, J. (n.d.). *World Employment Social Outlook: Trends for Women 2017*. International Labour Organization. file:///C:/Users/janellew/Downloads/wcms_557245.pdf

7. Charmes, J. (2019). *The Unpaid Care Work and the Labour Market. An analysis of time use data based on the latest World Compilation of Time-use Surveys*. International Labour Organization. https://www.ilo.org/wcmsp5/groups/public/@dgreports/@gender/documents/publication/wcm s_814499.pdf

8. Mahajan, D., White, O., Madgavkar, A., & Krishnan, M. (2020, September 16). *Don't let the pandemic set back gender equality*. Harvard Business Review. https://hbr.org/2020/09/dont- let-the-pandemic-set-back-gender-equality

9. Woetzel, L., Madgavkar, A., Ellingrud, K., Labaye, E., Devillard, S., Kutcher, E., Manyika, J., Dobbs, R., & Krishnan, M. (2015, September 1). *How advancing women's equality can add $12 trillion to global growth*. McKinsey & Company. https://www.mckinsey.com/featured-insights/employment-and-growth/how-advancing- womens-equality-can-add-12-trillion-to-global-growth

Chapter 2

1. Wharton, A. S. (1993). The affective consequences of service work: Managing emotions on the job. *Work and Occupation, 20*, 205-232.
2. Cropanzano, R., Weiss, H. M., & Elias, S. M. (2004). The impact of display rules and emotional labor on psychological well-being at work. In P. L. Perrewe & D. C. Ganster (Eds.), *Reseaerch in occupational stress and well being* (pp. 45-89). Elsevier.
3. Grandey, A., Diefendorff, J., & Rupp, D. E. (2013). *Emotional labor in the 21st century: Diverse Perspectives on Emotion Regulation at work*. Routledge Academic.
4. Hochschild, A. R. (1983). *The managed heart: Commercialization of human feeling*. University of California Press.
5. Morris, J. A., & Feldman, D. C. (1996). The dimensions, antecedents, and consequences of emotional labor. *Academy of Management Review, 21*, 986-1010.
6. Morris, J. A., & Feldman, D. C. (1997). Managing emotions in the workplace. *Journal of Managerial Issues*, 257-274.
7. Richards, J. M., & Gross, J. J. (1999). Composure at any cost? The cognitive consequences of emotion suppression. *Personality and Social Psychology Bulletin, 25*(8), 1033-1044.
8. Mayhew, C. (2002). Occupational violence in industrialized countries: Types, incidence patterns, and 'at risk' groups of workers. In M. Gill, B. Fisher, & V. Bowie (Eds.). *Violence at work: Causes, patterns and prevention.* (pp. 21-40). Willan Publishing.
9. Guy, M. E., & Newman, M. A. (2004). Women's jobs, men's jobs: Sex segregation and emotional labor. *Public Administration Review, 64*(3), 289-298.
10. Wingfield, A. H. (2010). Are some emotions marked "Whites only?" Racialized feeling rules in professional workplaces. *Social Problems, 57*(2), 251-268.
11. Pugliesi, K., & Shook, S. L. (1997). Gender, jobs, and emotional labor in a complex organization. In R. J. Erickson & B. Cuthbertson-Johnson (Eds.), *Social perspectives on emotion*, (pp. 283-316). JAI.
12. Gross, J. J., & John, O. P. (2003). Individual differences in two emotion regulation processes: Implications for affect, relationships, and well-being. *Journal of Personality and Social Psychology, 85*(2), 348.

13. Humphrey, N. M. (2022). Racialized emotional labor: An unseen burden in the public section. *Administration & Society, 54*(4), 741-758.

14. Mirchandani, K. (2002). Reforming organisations: Contributions of teleworking employees. In P. Jackson (Ed.), *Virtual working: Social and Organisational Dynamics, (pp. 77-91)*. Routledge.

15. Cross, T. L., Bazron, B. J., Dennis, K. W., & Isaacs, M. (1989, March). *Towards a culturally competent system of care: A monograph on effective services for minority children who are severely emotionally disturbed.* CASSP Technical Assistance Center, Georgetown University Child Development Center. https://spu.edu/-/media/academics/school-of-education/Cultural- Diversity/Towards-a-Culturally-Competent-System-of-Care-Abridged.ashx

16. House-Niamke, S., & Eckerd, A. (2021). Institutional injustice: How public administration has fostered and can ameliorate racial disparities. *Administration & Society, 53*(2), 305-324.

17. Grandey, A. A., Houston, L., & Avery, D. R. (2019). Fake it to make it? Emotional labor reduces the racial disparity in service performance judgments. *Journal of Management, 45*(5), 2163-2192.

18. Sloan, M. M., Evenson Newhouse, R. J., & Thompson, A. B. (2013). Counting on coworkers: Race, social support, and emotional experiences on the job. *Social Psychology Quarterly*, 76(4), 343-372.

19. Wingfield, A. H. (2010). Are some emotions marked" whites only"? Racialized feeling rules in professional workplaces. *Social Problems*, 57(2), 251-268.

20. Schaubroeck, J., & Jones, J. R. (2000). Antecedents of workplace emotional labor dimensions and moderators of their effects on physical symptoms. *Journal of Organizational Behavior, 21*, 163-83.

21. Mann, S. (2004). 'People-work': Emotion management, stress and coping. *British Journal of Guidance & Counselling, 32*(2), 205-221.

22. Saxton, M. J., Phillips, J. S., & Blakeney, R. N. (1991). Antecedents and consequences of emotional exhaustion in the airline reservations service sector. *Human Relations*, 44(6), 583- 595.

23. Maslach, C., Jackson, S. E., & Leiter, M. P. (1997). *Maslach burnout inventory*. Scarecrow Education.

Chapter 3

1. Bringé, A. (2021, May 3). *The rise of athleisure in the fashion industry and what it means for brands*. Forbes. https://www.forbes.com/sites/forbescommunicationscouncil/2021/05/03/the- rise-of-athleisure-in-the-fashion-industry-and-what-it-means-for-brands/

2. Demby, G. (2013, April 8). *How code-switching explains the world*. NPR. https://www.npr.org/sections/codeswitch/2013/04/08/176064688/how-code-switching- explains-the-world

3. Mayew, W. J., Parson, C. A., &Venkatachalam, M. (2013). Voice pitch and the labor market success of male chief executive officers. *Evolution and Human Behavior, 34*(4), 243-248.
4. Eagly, A. H. (1987). Reporting sex differences. *American Psychologist, 42*(7), 756-757.
5. Eagly, A. H., & Karau, S. J. (2002). Role congruity theory of prejudice toward female leaders. *Psychological Review, 109*(3), 573-598.
6. Wood, W., & Eagly, A. H. (2012). Biosocial construction of sex differences and similarities in behavior. *Advances in Experimental Social Psychology, 46*, 55-123.
7. Heilman, M. E. (2001). Description and prescription: How gender stereotypes prevent women's ascent up the organizational ladder. *Journal of Social Issues, 57*(4), 657-674.
8. Schein, V. E. (1973). The relationship between sex role stereotypes and requisite management characteristics. *Journal of Applied Psychology, 57*(2), 95.
9. Klofsted, C. A., & Anderson, R. C. (2018). Voice pitch predicts electability, but does not signal leadership ability. *Evolution and Human Behavior, 39*(3), 349-354.
10. Lindsey, G. (2023, July 16). *Vocal Fry: What it is, who does it, and why people hate it!* YouTube. https://www.youtube.com/watch?v=Q0yL2GezneU
11. Grant, A. (2014). *Give and take: Why helping others drives our success.* Penguin.

Chapter 4

1. Rock, D., & Grant, H. (2016). Why diverse teams are smarter. *Harvard Business Review*, https://hbr.org/2016/11/why-diverse-teams-are-smarter
2. Subramanian, S., & Washington, E. F. (2022, February 25). *Why flexible work is essential to your DEI strategy.* Harvard Business Review. https://hbr.org/2022/02/why-flexible-work-is- essential-to-your-dei-strategy
3. Bureau of Labor Statistics. (2023). *Productivity.* U.S. Bureau of Labor Statistics. https://www.bls.gov/productivity/#:~:text=Productivity%20increased%204.7%20percent%20i n,labor%20costs%20increased%207.0%20percent.
4. Halford, S., & Leonard, P. (1999). New identities. Professionalism, managerialism and the construction of self. In M. Exworthy & S. Halford (Eds.), *Professionals and the new managerialism in the public sector* (pp. 102-120). Open University Press.
5. Ashforth, B. E., & Mael, F. (1989). Social identity theory and the organization. *Academy of Management Review, 14*, 20-39.

6. Tajfel, H., & Turner, J. (1979). An integrative theory of intergroup conflict. In J. A. Williams & S. Worchel (Eds.), *The social psychology of intergroup relations* (pp. 33-47). Wadsworth.

7. Tajfel, H., & Turner, J. C. (1985). The social identity theory of intergroup behavior. In S. Worchel & W. G. Austin (Eds.), *Psychology of Intergroup relations* (2nd ed., pp. 7-24). Nelson-Hall.

8. Turner, J. C, & Oakes, P. J. (1989). Self-categorization theory and social influence. In P. B. Paulus (Ed.), *Psychology of group influence* (2nd ed., pp. 233-275). Erlbaum.

9. Ruiz, D. M. (2001). *The four agreements.* Amber-Allen Publishing.

Chapter 5

1. Detert, J. (2023, January 9). *Let's call quiet quitting what it often is: Calibrated contributing.* MIT Sloan Management Review. https://sloanreview.mit.edu/article/lets-call-quiet-quitting- what-it-often-is-calibrated-contributing/

2. Moss, J. (2021, February 8). *Beyond burned out.* Harvard Business Review. https://hbr.org/2021/02/beyond-burned-out

3. Rudolph, C. W., Katz, I. M., Lavigne, K. N., & Zacher, H. (2017). Job crafting: A meta- analysis of relationships with individual differences, job characteristics, and work outcomes. *Journal of Vocational Behavior*, *102*, 112-138.

4. Maslach, C., & Leiter, M. P. (2017). Understanding burnout: New models. In C. L. Cooper & J. C. Quick (Eds.). *The handbook of stress and health: A guide to research and practice*, (pp. 36-56). Wiley.

5. Quin, A. (2023, April 25). *The benefits of a marketing funnel and how to create an effective one.* Forbes. https://www.forbes.com/sites/forbesagencycouncil/2023/04/25/the-benefits-of-a- marketing-funnel-and-how-to-create-an-effective-one/

6. Benson, K. A. (1984). Comment on crocker's "an analysis of university definitions of sexual harassment." *Signs: Journal of Women in Culture and Society*, *9*(3), 516-519.

7. Fayankinnu, E. A. (2012). Female executives' experiences of contra-power sexual harassment from male subordinates in the workplace. *Bangladesh e-Journal of Sociology*, *9*(2).

8. Greenberg, J. (1987). A taxonomy of organizational justice theories. *Academy of Management Review*, *12*(1), 9-22.

9. Harrison, M. A., & Stephens, K. K. (2019). Shifting from wellness at work to wellness in work: Interrogating the link between stress and organization while theorizing a move toward wellness-in-practice. *Management Communication Quarterly*, *33*(4), 616-649.

10. Parks, K. M., & Steelman, L. A. (2008). Organizational wellness programs: A meta-analysis. *Journal of Occupational Health Psychology, 13*(1), 58-68.

11. Vercio, C., Loo, L. K., Green, M., Kim, D. I., & Beck Dallaghan, G. L. (2021) Shifting focus from burnout and wellness toward individual and organizational resilience. *Teaching and Learning in Medicine*, 33(5), 568-576.

12. Hertz, R. (1986). *More equal than others: Women and men in dual-career marriages*. University of California Press.

13. Pabilonia, S. W., & Vernon, V. (2023). Who is doing the chores and childcare in dual-earner couples during the COVID-19 era of working from home? *Review of Economics of the Household, 21*, 519-565.

14. Robinson, J., & Godbey, G. (2010). *Time for life: The surprising ways Americans use their time*. Penn State Press.

Chapter 6

1. Crenshaw, K. (1991). Mapping the margins: Intersectionality, identity politics, and violence against women of color. *Stanford Law Review*, 43, 1241-1199.

2. Crenshaw, K. (2009). Race, reform, and retrenchment. In L. Back and J. Solomos (eds)
   Theories of race and racism, a reader, (pp. 549-560). Routledge.

3. Correll, S. J., Benard, S., & Paik, I. (2007). Getting a job: Is there a motherhood penalty?.
   American Journal of Sociology, 112(5), 1297-1338.

4. Mom Project. (2024). *Find the right hire for your company.* The mom project. https://work.themomproject.com/

5. Moms FIrst. (2024). *It's time to put moms first.* Momsfirst.us. https://momsfirst.us/?source_id=1046013

6. Player, A., Randsley de Moura, G., Leite, A. C., Abrams, D., & Tresh, F. (2019). Overlooked leadership potential: The preference for leadership potential in job candidates who are men vs. women. *Frontiers in Psychology, 10*, 1-14.

7. Field, E., Krivkovich, A., Kugele, S., Robinson, N., & Yee, L. (2023, October 5). *Women in the workplace 2023*. McKinsey & Company. https://www.mckinsey.com/featured- insights/diversity-and-inclusion/women-in-the-workplace

8. Catalyst. (2022). *Women in management (quick take).* Catalyst. https://www.catalyst.org/research/women-in-management/

9. UN Women. (2021). *Women and girls left behind: Glaring gaps in pandemic response*. UN Women. https://data.unwomen.org/sites/default/files/documents/Publications/ glaring-gaps- response-RGA.pdf

10. Gonzales, M. (2022, February 17). *Nearly 2 million fewer women in labor force*. Society for Human Resource Management (SHRM). https://www.shrm.org/topics-tools/news/inclusion-   equity-diversity/nearly-2-million-fewer-women-labor-force

11. Collins, P. H., & Bilge, S. (2020). *Intersectionality*. John Wiley & Sons.

12. Weinfuss, J. (2021, October 11). *I want to be someone to look up to": WNBA star Brittney Griner tells her coming out story*. ESPN. https://www.espn.com/espn/print?id=32303735

13. Bowleg, L. (2012). The problem with the phrase *women and minorities:* intersectionality-an important theoretical framework for Public Health. *American Journal of Public Health, 102*(7), 1267-1273.

Chapter 7

1. Huang, J., Krivkovich, A., Starikova, I., Yee, L., & Zanoschi, D. (2023, October 5). *Women in the workplace 2019*. McKinsey & Company. https://www.mckinsey.com/featured- insights/gender-equality/women-in-the-workplace-2019

2. Heilman, M. E. (2001). Description and Prescription: How gender stereotypes prevent women's ascent up the organizational ladder. *Journal of Social Issues, 57*(4), 657-674.

3. Schein, V. E. (1973). The relationship between sex role stereotypes and requisite management characteristics. *Journal of Applied Psychology,* 57(2), 95-100.

4. Eagly, A. H., & Wood, W. (1982). Inferred sex differences in status as a determinant of gender stereotypes about social influence. J*ournal of Personality and Social Psychology, 43,* 915-928.

5. Diehl, A., & Dzubinski, L. M. (2023). *Glass walls: Shattering the six gender bias barriers still holding women back at work*. Rowman & Littlefield Publishers.

6. Ryan, M. K., & Haslam, S. A. (2005). The glass cliff: Evidence that women are over- represented in precarious leadership positions. *British Journal of Management, 16,* 81-90.

7. Ryan, M. K., & Haslam, S. A. (2007). The glass cliff: Exploring the dynamics surrounding the appointment of women to precarious leadership positions. *The Academy of Management Review*, 32, 549-572.

8. Ryan, M. K., Haslam, S. A., Hersby, M. D., & Bongiorno, R. (2011). Think crisis-think female: The glass cliff and contextual variation in the think manager-think male stereotype. *Journal of Applied Psychology*, 96, 470-484.

9. Kulich, C., Ryan, M. K., & Haslam, S. A. (2014). The political glass cliff: Understanding how seat selection contributes to the underperformance of ethnic minority candidates. *Political Research Quarterly*, 67, 84-95.

10. Galinsky, A. D., Hall, E. V., & Cuddy, A. J. C. (2013). Gendered races: Implications for interracial marriage, leadership selection, and athletic participation. *Psychological Science, 24*(4), 498-506.

11. Gündemir, S., Carton, A. M., & Homan, A. C. (2019). The impact of organizational performance on the emergence of Asian American leaders. *Journal of Applied Psychology, 104*(1), 107-122.

12. Cook, A., & Glass, C. (2014). Above the glass ceiling: When are women and racial/ethnic minorities promoted to CEO? *Strategic Management Journal, 35,* 1080-1089.

13. Wood, W., & Eagly, A. H. (2012). Chapter two-Biosocial Construction of Sex Differences and Similarities in Behavior. In J. M. Olson & M. P. Zanna (Eds.), *Advances in Experimental Social Psychology* (Vol. 46, pp. 55-123). Academic Press.

14. Ashby, J., Ryan, M. K., & Haslam, S. A. (2007). Legal work and the glass cliff: Evidence that women are preferentially selected to lead problematic cases. *William & Mary Journal of Women and the Law, 13,* 775-793.

15. Wicker, P., Cunningham, G. B., & Fields, D. (2019). Head coach changes in women's college soccer: An investigation of women coaches through the lenses of gender stereotypes and the glass cliff. *Sex Roles*, 81, 797-807.

16. Smith, A. E. (2014). On the edge of a glass cliff: Women in leadership in local government. *Public Organization Review, 14*, 477-496.

17. Morgenroth, T., Kirby, T. A., Ryan, M. K., & Sudkämper, A. (2020). The who, when, and why of the glass cliff phenomenon: A meta-analysis of appointments to precarious leadership positions. *Psychological Bulletin, 146*(9), 797.

18. Brass, D. J. (1985). Men's and women's networks: A study of interaction patterns and influence in an organization. *Academy of Management Journal, 28*(2), 327-343.

19. Ibarra, H. (1992). Homophily and differential returns: Sex differences in network structure and access in an advertising firm. *Administrative Science Quarterly*, 37, 422-447.

20. McGuire, G. M. (2000). Gender, race, ethnicity, and networks: The factors affecting the status of employees' network members. *Work and Occupations*, 27(4), 501-524.

21. Wolfers, J. (2015, March 2). *Fewer women run big companies than men named John.* The New York Times. https://www.nytimes.com/2015/03/03/upshot/fewer-women-run-big-companies-than-men-named-john.html

22. Boyle, M., & Green, J. (2023, April 25). *Works shift: Women CEOs (Finally) outnumber those named John.* Bloomberg. https://www.bloomberg.com/news/newsletters/2023-04- 25/women-ceos-at-big-companies-finally-outnumber-those-named-john

23. Crockett M. J. (2017). Moral outrage in the digital age. *Nature Human Behaviour, 1*, 769- 771.

24. Edmondson, A. C. (2018). *The fearless organization: Creating psychological safety in the workplace for learning, innovation, and growth.* Wiley.

25. Field, E., Krivkovich, A., Kugele, S., Robinson, N., & Yee, L. (2023, October 5). *Women in the workplace 2023.* McKinsey & Company. https://www.mckinsey.com/featured- insights/diversity-and-inclusion/women-in-the-workplace

Chapter 8

1. Vaccaro, A., Daly-Cano, M., & Newman, B. M. (2015). A sense of belonging among college students with disabilities: An emergent theoretical model. *Journal of College Student Development*, *56*(7), 670-686.

2. Systemic and structural racism: Definitions, examples, health damages, and approaches to dismantling. *Health Affairs, 41*(2). 171-178.

3. Belfield, C. (2021). *The economic burden of racism from the U.S. education system.* National Education Policy Center. https://nepc.colorado.edu/publication/cost-of-racism

4. Rucker, J. M. & Richeson, J. A. (2021) Toward an understanding of structural racism: implications for criminal justice. *Science, 374*(6565), 286–290.

5. Eagly, A. H. (1983). Gender and social influence. *American Psychologist, 38*, 971-981.

6. Eagly, A. H., & Karau, S. J. (2002). Role congruity theory of prejudice toward female leaders. *Psychological Review, 109*(3), 573.

7. Ex, C. T. G. M., & Janssens, J. M. A. M. (1998). Maternal influences on daughters' gender role attitudes. *Sex Roles, 38*, 171-186.

8. Human Rights Careers. (2024). *Advocacy 101: Types, examples, and principles.* Human Rights Careers. https://www.humanrightscareers.com/issues/advocacy-types-examples- principles/

9. Miller, J. B. (1991). Women and power. In J. V. Jordan, A. G. Kaplan, J. B. Miller, I. P. Stiver, & J. L. Surrey (Eds.) *Women's growth in connection.* The Guilford Press.

10. Eagly, A. H., & Wood, W. (1982). Inferred sex differences in status as a determinant of gender stereotypes about social influence. *Journal of Personality and Social Psychology, 43,* 915-928.

11. Dépret, E. F., & Fiske, S. T. (1993). Social cognition and power: Consequences of social structure as a source of control deprivation. In G. Weary, F. Gleicher, & K. Marsh (Eds.), *Control motivation and social cognition* (pp. 176-202). Springer-Verlag.

12. Hollander, E. P. (1985). Leadership and power. In G. Lindzey & E. Aronson (Eds.) *The handbook of social psychology* (Vol. 2, 3rd ed., pp. 485-537). Random House.

Our (In)visible Work
Chapter 9

1. Sabat, I. E., Martinez, L. R., & Wessel, J. L. (2013). Neo-activism: Engaging allies in modern workplace discrimination reduction. *Industrial and Organizational Psychology: Perspectives on Science and Practice, 6*, 480-485.

2. Radke, H. R. M., Kutlaca, M., Siem, B., Wright, S. C., & Becker, J. C. (2020). Beyond allyship: Motivations for advantaged group members to engage in action for disadvantaged groups. *Personality and Social Psychology Review, 24*(4), 291-315.

3. Salter, N. P., & Migliaccio, L. (2019). Allyship as a diversity and inclusion tool in the workplace. *Diversity within Diversity Management, 22*, 131-152.

4. Luthra, P., & Muhr, S. L. (2023). *Leading Through Bias: 5 Essentials Skills to Block Bias and Improve Inclusion at Work.* Palgrave Macmillan.

5. Hollander, E. P. (1985). Leadership and power. In G. Lindzey & E. Aronson (Eds.) *The handbook of social psychology* (Vol. 2, 3rd ed., pp. 485-537). Random House.

6. Kalina, P. (2020). Performative allyship. *Technium Social Science Journal, 11*, 478-481.

7. Kutlaca, M., & Radke, H. R. M. (2023). Towards an understanding of performative allyship: Definition, antecedents and consequences. *Social and Personality Psychology Compass*, 17(2), e12724.

8. Lloren, A., & Parini, L. (2017). How LGBT-supportive workplace policies shape the experience of lesbian, gay men, and bisexual employees. *Sexuality Research and Social Policy, 14*, 289-299.

9. Górska, P., Bilewicz, M., Winiewski, M., & Waszkiewicz, A. (2017). On old-fashioned versus modern homonegativity distinction: Evidence from Poland. *Journal of Homosexuality, 64*(2), 256-272.

10. Connley, C. (2020, August 24). *Over 80% of White employees see themselves as allies at work, but Black women and Latinas disagree.* CNBC. https://www.cnbc.com/2020/08/21/over-80percent-of-white-employees-see-themselves-as- allies-but-black-women-and-latinas-disagree.html

11. Piccigallo, J. R., Lilley, T. G., & Miller, S. L. (2012). It's cool to care about sexual violence: Men's experiences with sexual assault prevention. *Men and Masculinities, 15*(5), 507-525.

12. Ford, K. A., & Orlandella, J. (2015). The 'not-so-final remark': The journey to becoming white allies. *Sociology of Race and Ethnicity, 1*(2), 287-301.

13. Van Zomeren, M., Spears, R., & Leach, C. W. (2008). Exploring psychological mechanisms of collective action: Does relevance of group identity influence how people cope with collective disadvantage?. *British Journal of Social Psychology, 47*(2), 353-372.

14. Nittrouer, C. L., Hebl, M. R., Ashburn-Nardo, L., Trump-Steele, R. C., Lane, D. M., & Valian, V. (2018). Gender disparities in

colloquium speakers at top universities. *Proceedings of the National Academy of Sciences, 115*(1), 104-108.

15. Becker, A., Deckers, T., Dohmen, T., Falk, A., & Kosse, F. (2012). The relationship between economic preferences and psychological personality measures. *Annual Review of Economics, 4*(1), 453-478.

16. Droogendyk, L., Wright, S. C., Lubensky, M., & Louis, W. R. (2016). Acting in solidarity: Cross-group contact between disadvantaged group members and advantaged group allies. *Journal of Social Issues, 72*(2), 315-334.

17. Louis, K. S., & Murphy, J. F. (2019). Leadership for learning starts with relationships: The contribution of positive organizational studies. In J. Weinstein & G. Munoz (Eds.). *Leadership in schools under challenging circumstances*. Universidad Diego Portales.

18. Thomas, E. F., & McGarty, C. (2018). Giving versus acting: Using latent profile analysis to distinguish between benevolent and activist support for global poverty reduction. *British Journal of Social Psychology, 57*(1), 189-209.

Chapter 10

1. Padilla, A.M. (1994). Research news and comment: Ethnic minority scholars; research, and mentoring: Current and future issues. *Educational Researcher*, 23(4), 24-27.

www.ingramcontent.com/pod-product-compliance
Lightning Source LLC
Chambersburg PA
CBHW022054020426
42335CB00012B/690